Establishing a
Nature-Based Preschool

Rachel A. Larimore

interpPress

ISBN-13: 978-1-879931-30-5

NATIONAL ASSOCIATION FOR
INTERPRETATION

The National Association for Interpretation is a private nonprofit 501(c)(3) organization and professional association. NAI's mission is "Inspiring leadership and excellence to advance natural and cultural interpretation as a profession."

For information, visit www.interpnet.com.

On the cover: Photo by Holly Mahaffey.

To my parents—for providing me a childhood immersed in nature

Contents

Acknowledgements

This book is the result of the work and support of many, many people. Thank you to New Canaan Nature Center Preschool, Kalamazoo Nature Center's Nature's Way Preschool, Dodge Nature Preschool, and Schlitz Audubon Nature Center Preschool for being shining examples for others to emulate. Without the support of Chippewa Nature Center's (CNC) executive director Dick Touvell and board of directors, Nature Preschool would never have become a reality. The support of Alan Oman, Patti Bailie, Marcie Oltman, Gail Crosby, Missy Finney, and everyone at West Midland Family Center was also critical in getting this program up and running. Without their guidance I would have been a fish out of water. I hope I've been true to their guidance and leadership as I captured the steps to opening a new nature-based preschool program.

Writing the book itself involved much more than the author and computer. Thank you to my parents, Rick and Cloydia Larimore, for providing our family cabin as a place to escape and write and for editing—and then editing again. I'm very grateful for my other proofreaders—Dennis Pilaske, Alan Oman, Kendra Curtiss-Tomaski, and Patti Bailie. Thank you also to Tim Merriman, Paul Caputo, and the entire National Association for Interpretation (NAI) staff for their support of this project.

As I say throughout the book, the success of any preschool program is dependent on the teaching staff. I would be remiss not to acknowledge the CNC teaching staff. The magic that is created every day at CNC's Nature Preschool is due to the amazingly talented teachers. I am grateful every day for their passion, dedication, and drive.

Introduction

"Hey guys, over here! I found a gold mine!"

Not five minutes into his first day of Nature Preschool, this four-year-old boy had struck it rich! A gold mine? At preschool? His gold mine was a rotting log full of insects and other decomposers! This was just one of the many exciting moments on the first day of school in our new LEED-designed Nature Preschool building. The pride and excitement that came over all the staff on that September Monday morning in 2009 as children ran up the path to their beautiful new, sustainably designed Nature Preschool building was overwhelming.

It all began in late 2005 when the directors at Chippewa Nature Center (CNC), a private nonprofit nature center in Midland, Michigan, began discussing the need for a renovation and expansion of our nearly 20,000-square-foot visitor center. Prior to working at CNC, I worked at the Kalamazoo Nature Center in Kalamazoo, Michigan, and was impressed by their Nature's Way Preschool. I couldn't let go of what a powerful, age-appropriate, more intense educational experience this program was compared to the one-hour school programs or mom-and-tot programs nature centers so regularly offer. In fact, I was so impressed that the idea was constantly lingering in the back of my mind waiting to jump out when faced with the perfect moment. Discussions of a capital project seemed like the perfect time to broach the subject with the staff and board.

The leadership team at CNC was very open to the idea of a preschool, but of course there were many questions. Will this community support the program? Does it fit our mission? How much will it cost to get started? Will it break even? Generate a profit? And *many* more questions followed. We did have some information. We knew that other organizations such as Kalamazoo Nature Center in Michigan and New Canaan Nature Center in Connecticut had been running successful programs for many years. We also knew that newer programs were also quite successful. Among these were Schlitz Audubon Nature Preschool in Milwaukee, Wisconsin, and Dodge Nature Preschool in West Saint Paul, Minnesota. Then, in case that wasn't enough motivation to start discussing the topic, a book had just been published that was generating quite a buzz. Richard Louv's book, *Last Child in the Woods: Saving Our Children From Nature-Deficit Disorder*, brought the discussion to the forefront.

The successful examples of preschools at nature centers, the reminder by Richard Louv of the need to get children outside, and the plans for a major capital project all created our own positive "perfect storm" to begin seriously investigating the possibilities. I was given the go-ahead by our executive director, Dick Touvell, to meet with local stakeholders beginning in late summer 2006 about the feasibility of creating a new preschool program in our community. I sat down with Alan Oman, supervisor of early childhood and family services for Midland County Educational Services Agency. Alan provides training, resources, and coordination for many of the early childhood programs and services in the county. Dick Touvell and I met with Mrs. Margaret Ann Riecker of The Herbert H. and Grace A. Dow Foundation who, as part of a bigger feasibility study for the capital project, agreed to provide the funding for travel to visit other nature-based preschool sites. The ball was rolling, and picking up speed—quickly! By December I found myself boarding a plane to Minnesota with Dick Touvell and Alan Oman to begin what we affectionately referred to as the "Midwest Preschool Tour." When we landed in Minneapolis/Saint Paul the temperature was in the single digits. (To answer your next question, yes, the kids were playing outside that day—and they were smiling!)

Over the next three days we visited Dodge Nature Center and Tamarack Nature Center in the Minneapolis/Saint Paul area and then drove to Milwaukee where we visited the Schlitz Audubon Center. While in Milwaukee we met with The Kubala Washatko Architects (TKWA) who would become the architects of our new preschool building and visitor center renovation. From there we headed south around Lake Michigan and stopped for a visit at Kalamazoo Nature Center.

Alan gives a colorful explanation of the trip, but let's just say he had no idea what he was getting into when he agreed to go along. In fact, I'm almost positive he was thinking, "What in the world are these nature nuts doing getting into the preschool business?" By the time the Chicago skyline was in view, he was convinced that a nature-based preschool was just what our community needed. By the time we reached Kalamazoo we had a plan. We had a list of potential partners to schedule meetings with, potential locations for a pilot year, and a timeline of dates for getting board approval in order to open for fall. As I said, the ball was rolling—quickly!

This book is about the steps you need to take once you commit to the idea of starting a nature-based preschool. It's about defining what a nature-based preschool is. It's about articulating the need and purpose of a nature-based preschool. It's about the organizational impacts. It's about determining a location and the work necessary to make that location preschool-ready—including licensing. This book is about selecting a program format, promoting the new program in your community, hiring staff, and registering students. It's also about what it takes to make the program mission-based while also being developmentally appropriate for preschoolers and meeting the needs of the whole family.

Ultimately, the goal of this book is to share the many things I learned during the investigation phase, initial planning, and implementation of a preschool program. In no way do I claim to have learned all there is to know about starting a preschool. I also don't claim to know all there is to know about nature-based preschools. In fact, there are many amazing people in the nature-based preschool world to whom I owe a large debt of gratitude for their inspiration and guidance during this process. From these people and my own challenges and triumphs I have learned a great deal since we began this endeavor in mid-2006. I hope you'll be inspired and motivated to embark on your own nature-based preschool adventure and perhaps find your own gold mine. My goal in the next seven chapters is to provide you with a guide to make your journey a little bit easier.

1

Environmental Education and Early Childhood Education—A Natural Fit

Exposure to nature has been shown time and again to be critical to our physical, social, emotional, and intellectual health. With the knowledge that time in nature is beneficial to our well-being, you'd think outdoor activities would be a regular part of our lives—particularly our children's lives. Unfortunately, in recent years that has been far from the case.

The disconnect between nature and children is so significant that it prompted the book *Last Child in the Woods: Saving Our Children From Nature Deficit Disorder* by Richard Louv. It was this book, first published in 2005, that fueled the idea that had been burning at Chippewa Nature Center (CNC) to develop a nature-based preschool. Louv's book struck a chord with many, many people and has grown into a national movement to get children outside. One of the outcomes of that book and the resulting movement was the creation of the Children & Nature Network. In 2009, the Children & Nature Network generated a report titled *Children and Nature 2009: A Report on the Movement to Reconnect Children to the Natural World* that summarized accomplishments and research related to this movement to date and provides suggestions of how to move into the future. In the "What Can Educators Do" section of this report you'll find the following statement particularly relevant to our discussion about nature-based preschools:

> Support existing and new nature-themed schools, such as the Schlitz Audubon Nature Center Preschool, where, as the *Milwaukee Journal Sentinel* reported in April 2006, "a three-year-old can identify a cedar tree and a maple—even if she can't tell you what color pants she's wearing. And a four-year-old can tell the difference

HOLLY MAHAFFEY

Outdoor play develops a child's physical, social, and cognitive skills.

> between squirrel and rabbit tracks—even if he can't yet read any of the writing on a map. Young children learn through the sounds, scents, and seasons of the outdoors." Taking cues from the preschool's success in engaging children, an increasing number of nature centers are looking to add preschool programs not only to meet the demand for early childhood education but also to "create outdoor enthusiasts at a young age," the *Journal Sentinel* reported. And their success points to a doorway to the larger challenge—to better care for the health of the Earth.

That is a pretty direct and strong endorsement! The Schlitz program was one of the main models we used as we developed our program at CNC, and is highlighted in Chapter 2. Why would the Children & Nature Network make such a significant statement and endorsement of nature-based preschools? To answer this question completely we need to look at the philosophical roots of nature-based preschools.

A nature-based preschool combines environmental education with early childhood education to create meaningful outdoor experiences that are developmentally appropriate. The two main philosophical components are 1) developmentally appropriate (early childhood education) and 2) meaningful outdoor experiences (environmental education). First, let's look at these elements separately and then how, when joined together, they make something greater than the sum of their parts.

Early Childhood Education

Early childhood education (ECE) is the teaching of children from birth to eight years of age. In terms of grade level this is generally thought to span preschool, generally starting at age three, through first grade. It's key to point out that preschool is different than child care—even though both experiences may occur during early childhood years. ECE is an organized, theory-based practice that focuses on different developmental domains: social, emotional, cognitive, and physical. Generally, the goal of early childhood education, particularly preschool, is to prepare children to be successful in school and life, with kindergarten readiness as a common outcome. As with any true profession, early childhood education is supported by various professional associations such as the National Association for the Education of Young Children (NAEYC).

Environmental Education

The primary goal of environmental education is to change people's actions or behavior towards the environment, as a result of awareness, knowledge, attitude, and skills. In 1977, world leaders gathered and created what has become the foundation of environmental education, the *Declaration of the Tbilisi Intergovernmental Conference on Environmental Education*, which said:

> The goals of environmental education are: a) to foster clear awareness of, and concern about, economic, social, political and ecological interdependence in urban and rural areas; b) to provide every person with opportunities to acquire knowledge, values, attitudes, commitment, and skills needed to protect and improve the environment; and c) to create new patterns of behavior of individuals, groups, and society as a whole towards the environment.

CHIPPEWA NATURE CENTER

Nature-based preschools meet the goals of both early childhood and environmental education.

Unlike early childhood education, environmental education does not have a specific age range, but is directed at all ages—recognizing, of course, that programming is unique for each age group.

Environmental educators also are supported professionally through organizations like the North American Alliance for Environmental Education (NAAEE) and the National Association for Interpretation (NAI).

Early Childhood Education and Environmental Education Together

Early childhood education focuses on the first eight years of a child's life, a period of incredible growth, which includes their cognitive, physical, social, and emotional development. Environmental education aims to provide knowledge and skills, along with an emotional connection, to lead individuals to environmentally responsible behaviors. In a nature-based preschool students are meeting the goals of both early childhood and environmental education. They're building cognitive skills like divergent thinking as they generate ideas for the best fort design. They're building physical skills like balance, coordination, and endurance as they climb over rocks, carry logs, and hike trails. They're building their social and emotional skills while working with their peers and problem solving. While each discipline, early childhood education and environmental education, is strong in its own right, when combined in a nature-based preschool they are suddenly more powerful than the sum of their parts.

Cognitively, or intellectually, nature provides an ever-changing environment for children to explore and discover, engaging all of their senses, in order to build on their existing knowledge and experience. In nature children learn to observe the world around them, and then develop the ability to sort and classify. A prime example of this was a four-year-old boy who had two leaves in his hand and began to explain to me that one of the leaves was a red oak. I asked him how he knew and he said, "Look. It has pointed ends on the leaves." I then asked what the other leaf was, a leaf that had toothed edges. He examined the leaf a moment, and confidently turned to me and said, "A mohawk leaf." No, we don't have a new tree species in Michigan. This boy, however, was able to recognize the most significant characteristic of this leaf and how it differed from the oak leaf. He didn't know the "correct" name for the leaf, but recalled something else in life that has the same toothed characteristic, his favorite hairstyle, and related it to this situation. This simple leaf moment showed that he was building his cognitive skills in observation, sorting, classifying, and assimilation to previous knowledge.

There are many other cognitive outcomes of nature-based preschools as well, but perhaps the most significant cognitive benefit of early childhood education in nature

.Y MAHAFFEY

Loading a wagon provides learning opportunities for social skills such as cooperation, physical strength, and cognitive problem-solving skills—such as determining how to fit one more log on the load.

is the development of divergent thinking. This is a child's ability to creatively generate many different solutions to a problem. Many education philosophies emphasize divergent thinking. After all, the world is changing too quickly for us to know what problems our children will face 30 years from now. However, if we teach them creative problem solving we're giving them the tools to face whatever problem might arise. The ever-changing natural world and its "loose parts," a term coined by landscape architect Simon Nicholson, are perfect teachers of creativity. The examples are endless—creating a bridge across a puddle, designing a fort to protect their prized rock collection, building a "pond" in the sandbox that just doesn't want to hold water, and so forth.

Nature is also a teacher for a child's physical development. Daily outdoor play in a nature-based preschool is an ideal way for children to develop physically. Walking and running over uneven terrain, through a thick brushy understory, or around a squishy wetland all provide different opportunities for physical development—from sheer muscle strength to body control and balance. A wet log, that was dry yesterday, suddenly provides a new challenge for the child in terms of balance and coordination. Hikes with the entire class help build endurance in a fun and interesting way. Last, but far from least, is exactly what a local superintendent said when he visited Nature Preschool recently, "Well, *that* is the way to fight childhood obesity. Look at them running and jumping!"

In addition to cognitive and physical development, nature-based preschools enhance social and emotional development. Students develop their social and emotional skills by interacting, discovering, creating, and problem solving with other children and teachers. Imagine the conflicts that can arise when a group of children are building a fort, but that's exactly what early childhood is about—learning how to constructively resolve conflicts. It is in early childhood when a child's sense of wonder is at its peak. Nature provides endless opportunities for children to find wonder and in turn ask questions about the world around them. This helps build their intellectual capacity as we discussed above, but it also helps develop their confidence and sense of place in the world.

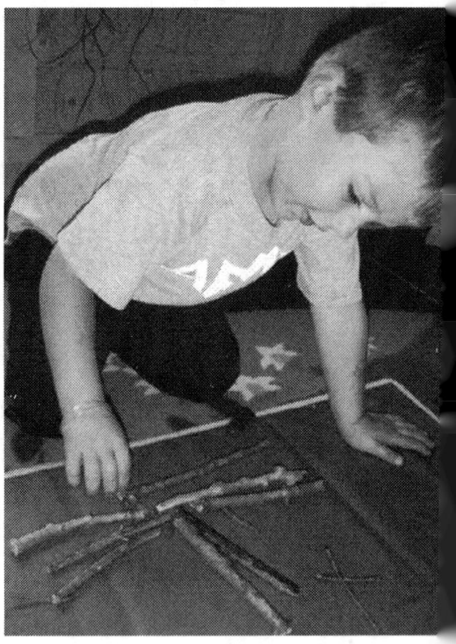
CHIPPEWA NATURE CENTER

Nature-based preschools are mission-based—developing a child's emotional connection to nature while at the same time developing their knowledge and skills.

Daily outdoor activities also develop a child's emotional connection to the natural world, which has been shown to be critical in influencing later adult behaviors toward environmental protection. Imagine the child who climbs the same tree day in and day out. If the tree were cut down the child would be devastated—not because someone told the child trees were important, but because that child developed a personal connection with that tree. That tree was important to that child. This is the development of emotional connections, which is at the core of environmental education. The ability to deal with the loss and express their feelings related to the loss is the concern of early childhood education.

It's the emotional connections and attitude development of environmental education along with the sensory- and play-based learning of early childhood that come together to form a powerful educational experience in a nature-based preschool—more powerful than either discipline is standing alone. It's these emotional connections that help develop a child's lifelong connection with the natural world.

I realize I've just summarized two significant professions, each with a long history, into a few paragraphs. I encourage you to delve into the scientific research supporting the joining of early childhood education and environmental education. See the research resource list in Appendix A.

Nature Center Perspective on Value of Nature-Based Preschools

Nature-based preschools are ideal programs for nature centers or interpretive centers. There are significant positive impacts directly related to achieving the mission of connecting people to nature along with potential financial benefits.

Earlier I discussed the power of combining early childhood and environmental education, and clearly this kind of program achieves the environmental education portion of the mission. However, I want to emphasize that achievement some more. A nature-based preschool provides outdoor experiences to children anywhere from two to five days per week for at least nine months at a time. That is far more time than a two-hour school field trip visit once per year; far more than a mom-and-tot program that happens once a month; and far more than even a week-long summer day camp program. Please do not misunderstand—I am not saying those programs aren't valuable. I am, however, saying that the quality and length of outdoor time in a nature-based preschool program has a significantly greater impact on the organizational mission of any nature center. This immersion in nature early in life will develop a child's lifelong connection to the natural world.

In addition to being a potentially fiscally rewarding endeavor, nature-based preschools are a very mission-rich program. From a financial perspective, most of the nature-based preschools currently operating as part of a nature center are not only breaking even, many are actually generating a profit. That's a rare program characteristic in the nature center world. For most of our programs, what visitors are willing to pay is far less than the actual cost of the program. Preschool is a very different kind of service, which changes the payment discussion significantly. Keep in mind that each program and community is unique. The decisions you make related to all aspects of setting up your program will impact the profit margin greatly. In other words, while the program has the potential to generate profit, there are many factors at play.

The other financial benefit of an on-site nature-based preschool is that it can strengthen your membership base (also called "friends" at some organizations). First of all, you're attracting families from all around the community that might not otherwise be regular visitors, let alone become members. This is done by either a) requiring membership to register, or b) building the cost of membership into their tuition so every family automatically becomes a member. Families build a strong connection with the nature center after visiting multiple times each week for months at a time. That results in families wanting to stay connected with the organization after the children have left preschool. As we all know, a strong membership base can also lead to a strong donor base. Also consider the community members without children, but who love the program idea and choose to support it.

Nature-based preschools are a programming gem. Yes, there are limitations of facilities, community need, start-up costs, etc., and this book is intended to help nature centers decide if this program is feasible. However, in a perfect world there is no reason why a nature center shouldn't embrace nature-based preschools—they're everything we could ever hope a program to be.

2

What is a Nature-Based Preschool?

In recent years the term *nature-based preschool* has come to be associated with preschool programs that are typically owned and operated by a private, nonprofit nature center. The programs emphasize daily outdoor experiences and kindergarten-readiness in the context of nature and science education. This is a licensed early childhood program that meets over the course of a school year. This is a more regular, long-term program akin to traditional preschool and should not be confused with the mom-and-tot kinds of early childhood programs offered by many nature centers. (By the way, don't abandon your drop-in early childhood programs—they have a great educational value and are a great marketing tool and feeder program for your new preschool!)

However, simply being administered by a nature center doesn't make a preschool nature-based. Just having a preschool on nature center property doesn't necessarily make it nature-based either. Obviously having an organizational philosophy centered on teaching about nature and a facility with a great deal of natural features gives a nature center an advantage, but it doesn't automatically make the program nature-based. I also want to be very clear that a preschool can be nature-based without being associated with a nature center. In fact, if we limit nature-based preschools to nature centers we'll be doing a huge disservice to our children. *Any preschool in this country, or world for that matter, can be nature-based. There is no reason a private, for-profit preschool couldn't also be nature-based.*

If any program can be nature-based what really defines a "nature-based preschool?" First of all, children are outside every day unless the weather is dangerous. Dangerous means lightning, severe cold, etc. This should be clear—it is assumed by our teachers and

CHIPPEWA NATURE CENTER

It is common in the fall and spring for the entire class time of a nature-based preschool session to be held outside—including rest time.

parents that we'll be outside *every* day. In the four years we've been open there have only been three days or so where we couldn't go outside for at least a few minutes. This is an essential point and to be effective has to be deeply rooted in the organizational philosophy. It is especially critical when hiring staff as it is their attitude that will make or break this practice. We often have parents come to open houses and say, "We were told at another school that licensing won't allow children outside if it's below freezing." In Michigan there is no defined minimum temperature, so I know that these programs aren't going outside because the staff doesn't want to get cold and/or the children aren't properly dressed for the weather.

These daily outdoor experiences should connect children to the natural world around them—to the natural features around your facility. If there is a pond nearby the kids should be visiting that pond so often that they know every frog's secret hideout. In order to connect with their natural surroundings the activities and explorations should be centered on what is happening seasonally. For example, we spend late February and early March tapping maple trees to make maple syrup. During this time of year we take the kids, every day, to check the sap buckets. These regular experiences and seasonal connections help create a sense of place and belonging.

There are many ways a nature-based preschool is similar to a traditional preschool. The programs fall under all of the same state licensing regulations, there is a snack time, and group meeting time. As in a traditional preschool program, there is indoor choice time in the classroom. However, in a nature-based program, every indoor area is infused with nature. At Chippewa Nature Center, you'll find seed and rock collections in our discovery area. You'll find kid-sized butterfly wings, backpacks, and field jackets in our play area. Our library area is full of books that have nature themes. Our music area includes squirrel and turkey calls in addition to the traditional guitars and drums. In a nature-based preschool the outdoor learning does not stop when the children cross the building's threshold. Let me say that one more time so it doesn't get missed: *In a nature-based preschool the outdoor learning does not stop when the children cross the building's threshold.*

History of Nature-Based Preschools

Nature-based preschools have become quite the hot topic in the last few years. However, this type of program is not a new idea at all. In fact, New Canaan Nature Center in Connecticut has had a program since 1967 and Kalamazoo Nature Center in Michigan has been operating its nature-based preschool program since 1982. For years both of these programs served as the shining examples of what a preschool program at a nature center could be. In September 2000, Dodge Nature Center in West Saint Paul, Minnesota, opened a brand new, state-of-the-art facility with three classrooms. Shortly thereafter, in 2003, the Schlitz Audubon Nature Preschool in Milwaukee, Wisconsin, opened its doors as part of the newly built visitor center. These four programs, in particular, have been incredible models and inspirations to the nature center world. Their success and the reminders from Richard Louv's book *Last Child in the Woods* seemed to spark a new fire among nature centers to begin their own nature-based preschool program. In fact, that's exactly what led to the creation of CNC's Nature Preschool. We were very fortunate to have great models in the programs mentioned above, and amazing support as we began our program.

CHIPPEWA NATURE CENTER

At a nature-based preschool there's no such thing as bad weather—just bad clothing.

A Few Shining Examples

While there are now more than 20 nature-based preschools nationwide, there are some programs that stand out among the small but growing crowd. Some are long-standing programs and some very new in comparison. Unfortunately the things that make these programs really stand out are nearly impossible to put on paper. As I'll talk about in later chapters, it's the program philosophy and staff that make a program excel. All of the programs I'll mention focus on discovery-based, child-driven, experiential education. There is so much to learn from all of these programs. If at all possible, I encourage you to visit some of them prior to opening your program. For our discussion here I'll focus on the basic overview of the program and things they are doing that is unique to them.

New Canaan Nature Center Preschool

New Canaan Nature Center Preschool, established in 1967, is by far the longest running nature-based preschool in the country. This program, formerly called Beginner's Nature Program, is part of the New Canaan Nature Center's spectacular 40-acre campus just north of downtown New Canaan, Connecticut. New Canaan, one of the most affluent communities in the country, has a population of approximately 20,000 nestled in a county of more than 900,000 residents. The New Canaan Nature Center (NCNC) is a private, nonprofit organization. The classrooms are in buildings remaining from the old estate that was on the property, which have been renovated to meet childcare licensing requirements.

NEW CANAAN NATURE CENTER

New Canaan Nature Center Preschool, New Canaan, Connecticut

The preschool program serves approximately 100 students each year in a four-classroom facility. There are three- to five-year old programs offered in single age classrooms. The three-year-old programs have a student-teacher ratio of 14:2, where the four-year-old programs have a ratio of 16:2, and the five-year-old program is 18:3. The teachers are trained in early childhood education, child development, and environmental education. Each classroom is also partnered with an environmental educator from the nature center staff. This educator joins the class on guided hikes, brings live animals into the classroom, and is a resource for the class on natural history related questions.

Program offerings for 2011–12 school year

Program	Ages served[1]	Session length	Capacity	Student/ Teacher Ratio	Scholarships Available	NAEYC[2] Accredited
Chippewa Nature Center's Nature Preschool, Midland, MI (Program Est. 2007)	3- to 4-year-olds (mixed & single age classes)	3 hours; 2–4 days per week	88	16:3 (3-year-olds); 18:3 (mixed age)	Yes	No (Plan to start process in 2012)
Dodge Nature Preschool, Dodge Nature Center, West St. Paul, MN (Program Est. 2000)	3- to 5-year-olds (mixed age classes)	2.75 hours; 2, 3, or 5 days per week	190	18:3	Yes	Yes
Nature's Way Preschool, Kalamazoo Nature Center, Kalamzoo, MI (Program Est. 1982)	3- to 4-year-olds (classes by age group)	2.5 hours (3-year-olds); 3 hours (4-year-olds); 2 or 3 days per week	70	15:3 (3-year-olds); 20:3 (4-year-olds)	Yes	No
New Canaan Nature Center Preschool, New Canaan, CT (Program Est. 1967)	3- to 5-year-olds (classes by age group)	3 hours; 2-5 days per week	92	14:2 (3-year-olds); 16:2 (4-year-olds); 18:3 (5-year-olds)	Yes	Yes
Schilitz Audubon Nature Center Preschool, Milwaukee, WI (Program Est. 2003)	3- to 5-year-olds (mixed & single age classes)	2.75 hours; 2, 3, or 4 days per week	144	16:2 (plus a classroom volunteer)	Yes	In progress (Expected completion 2012)

1. All children must have independent bathroom skills at the start of school.
2. NAEYC is the National Association for the Education of Young Children

Starting in 2011–12, all of the three- and four-year-old class sessions will be three hours long with options of two to five days per week. The three-year-old programs have the option to add an afternoon session to their week for the last half of the school year. An additional three-year-old class will begin in January for the youngest students. The five-year-old program will be offered five days per week with two days being three hours long and the other three days being five hours long. An optional lunchtime program will also be available for an additional fee. This is a 60- to 90-minute before- or after-school activity for children ready to extend their day. While the program is driven by tuition, they do offer financial assistance to those families that have a financial need. Assistance is typically 10 to 30 percent of tuition and is awarded to approximately five percent of the students in the program.

The New Canaan Nature Center Preschool uses the Connecticut Preschool Curriculum Framework to guide program planning and student assessment. The program is accredited by the National Association for the Education of Young Children (NAEYC). This accreditation is a rigorous evaluation process to ensure that the program adheres to the best practices in early childhood education.

Kalamazoo Nature Center's Nature's Way Preschool

Nature's Way Preschool, located in Kalamazoo, Michigan, has been owned and operated by Kalamazoo Nature Center since 1982. The preschool is located about 15 minutes from the main nature center site in the city of Kalamazoo on a nine-acre natural area with woods, wetlands, and a stream running through. The cities of Kalamazoo and neighboring Portage have a combined population of about 120,000.

Kalamazoo Nature Center's Nature's Way Preschool, Kalamazoo, Michigan

One classroom, held in a log cabin, and one play area allows for half-day sessions two or three days per week for three- and four-year-olds. With a ratio of 15 students to three teachers in the three-year-old class and 20:3 in the four-year-old class, the program has the capacity to serve 70 children. Nature's Way Preschool is a tuition-based program, but also offers scholarships to those students that qualify based on family income. Approximately 15 percent of the students receive financial assistance.

Nature's Way's location away from the main Kalamazoo Nature Center means that a more conscious effort is placed on connecting families to the nature center. As a result, naturalists visit the classroom regularly and classes take monthly field trips to the main nature center property. At the end of a child's schooling at Nature's Way, the children, their families, and their teachers have an overnight campout experience at the nature center to celebrate moving on to kindergarten.

Looking to the future, Nature's Way has been selected to be part of a pilot program, Kalamazoo County Ready 4s, which is intended to soon provide a high-quality preschool program for all four-year-olds in the county. Nature's Way is building on this opportunity by committing to expanding the classroom facilities and natural play area.

Dodge Nature Center's Preschool

Dodge Nature Preschool is owned and operate by the private nonprofit Dodge Nature Center, located in West Saint Paul, Minnesota. The preschool opened its doors to a three-classroom program in September 2000. The preschool is located on the main 110-acre nature center property, several hundred yards from main center office and even closer to the farm education building. As part of the greater Minneapolis-Saint Paul community the preschool draws from a population of more than 3 million people.

The Dodge Nature Preschool program is accredited by the National Association for the Education of Young Children (NAEYC). Serving more than 190 children each year in this high-quality program, Dodge offers half-day, mixed-age sessions for three- to five-year olds. These sessions are two hours and 45 minutes long and are offered two, three, or five days per week. All of these sessions have a maximum of 18 students with three teaching staff.

DODGE NATURE CENTER

Dodge Nature Center Preschool, West Saint Paul, Minnesota

Dodge has had great success with its Lunch Bunch program. This program is one hour and 15 minutes long where children bring their lunch from home and can have additional play time with their friends either before or after their class session. There is a charge for the program, which provides additional revenue to the preschool. Typically 15 percent of the students participate in the Lunch Bunch program. This program is staffed to maintain a ratio of one teacher to every 10 children.

In order to spread the word about nature-based preschools and nature-based education in general, Dodge Nature Preschool now offers a one-day teacher training in the spring. This gives teachers from other programs an opportunity to learn about nature-based early childhood education and observe the program in action. As another outreach effort, the staff at Dodge Nature Preschool wrote and published a book, *Four Seasons at a Nature-Based Preschool*, which is a must-have resource manual for any preschool looking to integrate nature into their program. (See Appendix B for ordering information.)

Schlitz Audubon Nature Center Preschool

Schlitz Audubon Nature Center Preschool was established in 2003 to serve three- to five-year-olds. The program started with two classrooms built specifically for preschoolers as part of the new construction of the main visitor center. Located on the shore of Lake Michigan in a northern Milwaukee, Wisconsin, neighborhood, the preschool draws from a population of more than 950,000. The center's 185 acres provides lots of space for preschoolers to make discoveries in different ecosystems.

Half-day class sessions, which have a 15-minute staggered start to ease traffic congestion at arrival and departure times, are offered for two hours and 45 minutes. Families choose two, three, or four days per week. Classes have 16 children with a maximum ratio of one teacher to every eight children. The program has grown to three classrooms because of the demand for the program. In order to better accommodate the indoor and overall program expansion, they now have three outdoor play areas. This allows each class to begin its day in one of the outdoor play areas without the competition of another class. These facility changes have allowed the program's capacity to grow to 144 students. It should be noted that Schlitz Nature Preschool has been at full capacity every year of its operation.

SCHLITZ AUDUBON NATURE CENTER

Schlitz Audubon Nature Center Preschool, Milwaukee, Wisconsin

The Schlitz Nature Preschool has also created an after-school program to extend the preschool experience for alumni children from kindergarten to third grade. This program, Nature Adventurers, is offered weekly for five weeks each season, and helps keep children and families connected to the center well after their preschool experience has ended.

Schlitz Nature Preschool has developed a unique partnership with two local inner-city childcare centers. These centers visit the Schlitz Nature Preschool regularly throughout the school year (either every other week or once monthly), use one of the preschool classrooms, and are taught by one of the Schlitz teachers. As a result, these childcare centers are really considered part of the Schlitz Nature Preschool program and family. The Schlitz staff also visits these childcare centers once a month and provides them with a nature-based curriculum trunk with the materials for the childcare providers to use in their classrooms throughout the month.

In partnership with BrainInsights, the Schlitz Audubon Center has also created a set of activity cards that provide nature-based activities to help develop a child's brain, called *Naturally Developing Young Brains*. Each card has an activity on one side and a simply stated brain development fact on the other. (See Appendix B for ordering information.)

Chippewa Nature Center's Nature Preschool

Chippewa Nature Center's (CNC) Nature Preschool was established in 2007 in Midland, Michigan. CNC is a private, nonprofit nature center based in a town of approximately 40,000 people. In the first two years the program was held in an existing building on the nature center property with one classroom. Initially, half-day classes were offered two and a half hours per day morning and afternoon, four days per week. In the second year classes were extended to three hours. In the third year, the program moved to a new facility built specifically for preschool, which included two classrooms.

CHIPPEWA NATURE CENTER

Chippewa Nature Center's Nature Preschool, in Midland, Michigan, is housed in the Margaret Ann Riecker Nature Preschool Building

Since that time the program offerings have included 1) a full-day class operating four days per week for four-year-olds only and 2) half-day classes morning and afternoon for two, three or four days per week. However, due to greater demand, only three-hour half-day sessions will be offered in 2011–12, allowing for a capacity of 88 children. Now registering for its fifth year, younger siblings of former students and the power of word of mouth are clearly big forces in filling the program. Each mixed-age classroom has three educators with a maximum of 18 children. The three-year-old program has a student-teacher ratio of 16:3. The program uses Creative Curriculum® for its curriculum and Teaching Strategies Gold® for its child assessment.

This program has a unique partnership with another local nonprofit organization, the West Midland Family Center, which allows some children in the program to be funded through the state of Michigan's Great Start Readiness Program (GSRP). GSRP is a program through Michigan's Department of Education designed to help at-risk four-year-old children receive a year of preschool education prior to kindergarten. By joining forces the two organizations were able to offer a unique nature-based program to at-risk children in the Midland area. Through this program, nine children in the full-day class receive a full scholarship. As a result of replacing the full-day class with two half-day sessions, 18 children will receive full scholarships. The rest of the program at CNC is tuition-based with some partial scholarships available based strictly on income. Currently the program is made up of approximately 60 percent full-paying tuition spots and 40 percent that receive some sort of assistance, with the extent of assistance varying greatly between families.

3

Getting Started

(or "Are we really going to do this?!")

If you're anything like me, there will probably be a day shortly after you've convinced yourself the nature-based preschool concept is worth pursuing, where you'll have a sudden overwhelming feeling of, "There's so much to do, where do I start?" Let me assure you that this feeling does eventually subside. You'll find that the next few steps won't necessarily come in a particular order. Some things may happen simultaneously or you may find you have to start on one step, skip to another, and then come back to the first. My best advice is to be patient.

There will be days where you feel like you're making no progress, but the more discussions and the more "soak time" people have about the concept, the closer you are to success. For me the entire project had a snowball effect—in the beginning it felt like it was moving very slowly, but it kept getting faster and faster and before I knew it, we were registering for our fourth year of classes and hosting an event for alumni. Let's turn to getting your snowball rolling now, shall we?

Gaining Support

Before you can get much further than reading this book, you'll need to start gaining the support of the other staff and board of directors of your organization. At Chippewa Nature Center, the first step was getting the support of our executive director, Dick Touvell. With his support and encouragement I was able to start having exploratory conversations with local preschool stakeholders, do preliminary research on the value and need of such a program in our community, and eventually complete a few visits to nature-based preschool sites. After we had gained a little more knowledge, felt the program was worth pursuing, and had a preliminary plan in place, we took the concept to the board of directors for approval of a pilot year.

In our presentation to the board of directors we provided a written document that included the following elements:

1. Overview of nature-based preschools and research done to date
2. Measures of success (mission, strategic plan, etc.)
3. Value of nature-based preschools (summary of the research)
4. List of existing nature-based preschools (including location and years of operation)
5. The local preschool market
6. Market potential (projections for future preschool attendance)
7. Proposed model (number of students, ages, location, etc.)
8. Timeline for implementation
9. Budget implications (short and long-term)
10. Additional resources including:
    a. Research related to nature-based preschools
    b. Insights from visits to other nature-based preschools
    c. List of preschools in our county
    d. Information related to the state-funded program (This may or may not be relevant for you. You might also consider federal programs such as Head Start. If you choose to follow a unique format or partnership include as much relevant information here for the board as possible while keeping it in a succinct and easily digestible form.)
    e. National statistics related to early childhood education
    f. State and local statistics (number of preschool children, income levels, etc.)

Fortunately at CNC we have a board that has a strong understanding of environmental education and the need to get our children outside while at the same time being fiscally responsible. Once we had done our homework it was very straightforward to lay out the facts for the board and get approval to move ahead. At another nature center the executive director was able to find one board member who was passionate about the idea and involve him in all of the initial research and discussions. This person was able to be a spokesperson on the board of directors. There is no surefire approach for convincing your board. No matter what, the more information and facts you have, the better off you'll be.

Remember, this is an area where you already have the knowledge and skills to be successful. Whether you're the executive director, the education director, or in some other role at your organization, you know who the point person on staff should be. You also know what kind of information the board is going to need to make a decision, when that information should be available, and how that information should be presented. Don't sell yourself short here. You've been successful in your organization to this point, why would this project be any different? Trust your gut and the precedent of what has worked in the past when you've started a new program.

Community Need and Support

One big question you'll have to answer is, "Will our community support a new preschool program?" The answer may be complicated. One factor is sheer number of preschoolers, another is the socio-economic makeup of the community. You'll also need to be aware of political ramifications related to your competition and the community as a whole.

To begin, I strongly recommend identifying one or two key local stakeholders who are experts in early childhood education in your community and schedule a face-to-face meeting with them. This may be a local consortium for preschools, the school superintendent, or a consultant who works with and observes local programs. If you're really struggling to find someone, call the person responsible for the licensing of preschools and daycare centers in your area. This person should be able to give you the names of preschool leaders in the community.

When you have your first meeting with the stakeholder(s) you'll want to simply state what a nature-based preschool is and why you'd like to start one in your community. Then explain that you're meeting with them to help determine if the program would be viable in your community. Then, let them do the talking. Be sure to get information on the number of programs offered in your community. Have there been recent openings or closings of programs and why? Are there any community initiatives underway related to preschool? How are most of the programs funded—tuition-based, cooperatives, state funded, grant supported, etc.? There is a lot of information to gather, but if you find the right person in your community they should be able to easily answer these questions.

In the case of CNC, I started by talking with Alan Oman, the supervisor of early childhood and family services for Midland County. Essentially Alan's job is to coordinate county-wide early-childhood efforts. It seemed reasonable that he would have a good sense of the community need and if the community could accommodate a new and unique program like we were proposing. Initially it was simply a conversation with two primary goals: 1) I wanted him to understand the idea we were proposing and why; and 2) I wanted to get a sense from him if the community could accommodate a nature-based preschool. At first Alan was skeptical. He understood the need to get kids outside, but how was this program going to be different from any other preschool program that went outside regularly for preschool? I sent him a few written resources, including links to other nature-based preschool programs, and gave him a little "soak time" as I described earlier.

We met again a couple of months later to discuss the concept again. This time we also included the superintendent of our local school district, whose insight was quite valuable. His perspective was important because the state distributes some funds directly to school districts to operate or contract out the operation of preschool programs. I explained the concept and value of a nature-based preschool, and I received additional insight into the preschool component of our community. By the end of this meeting we decided it would be valuable to visit other nature-based preschools to see them in operation. I'll discuss site visits more later in this chapter, but let me say now that you should make sure local stakeholders go with you on site visits. Alan decided to go along on the trip so he had a strong knowledge of the kind of program we were proposing. His presence on the trip was invaluable. Nature-based preschools are very different from traditional preschools, so seeing them in person is very helpful in fully understanding the concept.

With the endorsement of these key stakeholders, we were able to gain the confidence and support of West Midland Family Center (WMFC), and convince them to partner with us on the new endeavor. WMFC is a private nonprofit that provides educational and recreational opportunities to community residents. WMFC also has more than 20 years experience operating preschools and is one of the most experienced Great Start Readiness Program grantees in the state. The partnership with WMFC added instant preschool credibility. (I should mention that we had worked with WMFC quite a bit in the past, so we had a successful partnership history. Without that I don't think the Family Center would have been so willing to work with us.) This partnership allowed us to be accessible to families from all income levels. In the end, we invested a great deal of time—several months, in fact—getting to know our local stakeholders, building trust among these groups, and visiting other sites. Without that investment we likely wouldn't have been successful in our presentation to the board of directors and definitely wouldn't have been successful in the community.

In gaining support from local stakeholders, you ultimately want people who are as passionate as you are about the concept. Ideally you're creating a team of allies who will help your program be successful. Just like gaining support from board of directors, you have the skills and contacts to make this happen. The key is to be able to clearly and succinctly explain what a nature-based preschool is and why you'd like to start one in your community. From there, do a lot of listening and remember that everyone wants their community to have the best opportunities available for its children—and a nature-based preschool fits that description.

In addition to meeting with local stakeholders, gather basic data on the number of preschool programs in your community. How many programs are there? Who provides the programs—for-profits, churches, etc.? What is the makeup of each program—half day versus full day, ages served, timing, etc.? How much do the programs cost? Are there any local, state, or federal funding sources you should be aware of? I also suggest gathering basic census data on the county related to the number of preschool children and projected future numbers. Family income levels in your community are also important factors when it comes to establishing tuition rates. In our report to the board of directors we also included national statistics related to early childhood education such as the number of children enrolled in preschool and the average time children spend in a day care center. One resource for these kinds of national statistics is the National Institute for Early Education Research (www.nieer.org). Before committing financial resources to a new program your board will likely want to see these kinds of statistics.

As you can see, "Will our community support a new preschool program?" involves lots of factors—making it a really tricky question to answer.

Visiting Other Nature-Based Preschool Sites

Visiting other nature-based preschool sites will be a key factor in your success. You may even need to go on multiple visits—once with your stakeholders in the decision-making process and later with your teaching staff. Reading about a nature-based preschool or even talking to staff at those programs does not compare with seeing the program in action. If possible, try to schedule a short tour of a few programs. When we began discussions of a preschool at CNC, we went on a "Midwest Tour of Preschools" that included Dodge and Tamarack Nature Centers in Minnesota, Schlitz Audubon Center in Wisconsin, and Kalamazoo Nature Center in Michigan. By visiting more than one program you'll get an idea of the variations and options available within the basic nature-based preschool concept.

To set up a visit call ahead, a few weeks in advance if possible, and make arrangements with the preschool director. You'll want a short tour of the facilities and then be able to meet with the director and ask specific questions. If there are resources you know you're going to ask for, let the director know when you schedule the visit. That way materials can be gathered prior to your arrival. Also, when you're setting up the visit, ask the director if you may take photos. For the children's privacy and safety many preschools will not allow you to take photos of the children. However, most will allow you to photograph the facilities. If so, take *lots* of pictures as they'll come in handy when you're talking with stakeholders and later when you're designing your classroom.

I also highly recommend having a list of questions prepared ahead of time. Take the list with you on the visit and take copious notes. Trust me, you won't remember everything and there will be lots of things to remember. Here are a few suggestions of questions to ask and things to look for:

- Program history
- What are the class offerings (ages, days of the week, length of the program, etc.)?
- How is the program funded (part of the umbrella organization, tuition, grants, fundraisers, etc.)?
- How do the families pay (full tuition, cooperative, tuition on a sliding scale, scholarships, etc.)?
- Do families typically pay monthly or for the entire year?
- Does the program offer discounts of any kind (e.g., payment for entire year, multiple children in the program)?
- Program:
    - What is the schedule for a typical day?
    - Are snacks and/or meals served? If so, how is that done?
    - What is the curriculum used in the classroom (e.g., self-developed, Creative Curriculum, Reggio-Emilia, Montessori, HighScope)?
    - What kind of child assessment is done?
    - What kind of overall program evaluation is done?
    - Is the program accredited?
    - What programs do you offer outside of the regular class (e.g., parent orientations, home visits, family nights, resources that are sent home with families)?
    - What relationships do you have with local schools? Is there a formal process to help transition students to kindergarten?

- Facilities:
    - What are the different areas inside the classroom(s)?
    - Is there additional indoor space besides the classroom(s)?
    - Where are the restrooms located? How many?
    - Where are the children's cubbies located?
    - Where do parents sign in every day?
    - How many outdoor play areas are there?
    - What is the children's favorite feature in the outdoor play area? Least favorite?
    - What is the staff's favorite thing about the facility?
    - What would the staff like to change about the facility?
- Staffing:
    - What is the staff-to-student ratio?
    - What are the minimum qualifications of staff?
    - What are the procedures for interviewing staff?
    - Who handles the clerical and administrative aspects of the program?
    - How are other staff members from the organization involved in the preschool program?
- Parent involvement:
    - How often do parents volunteer in the classroom? Are they required to?
    - How else do you involve parents in the program?
    - How often are parent-teacher conferences held and when?
    - Do you have a parent advisory group? If so, how does that operate?

You'll want to ask for these materials as well:

- Marketing brochures and flyers
- Registration form
- Scholarship application (if applicable)
- Parent handbook
- Policies and procedures manual
- Job descriptions for teachers
- Any other written resources available to parents and/or the public

Keep in mind that, with a limited number of nature-based preschools in existence, the preschools you're visiting probably get a lot of visitors over the course of a school year. In fact, don't be surprised if the school has designated tour days. Be respectful of their time and appreciative that they're willing to sit down and help you. Remember—treat others as you would like to be treated because soon you'll have people wanting to visit *your* preschool!

Establishing a Philosophy

Early on in the process of creating your nature-based preschool you should establish a written program philosophy. A simply written mission statement specific to the preschool program and a general philosophy statement will help you to stay focused as you begin planning and making programming decisions. These statements don't need to be elaborate, but they need to clearly state your program goals. Below are the statements we use at CNC. Notice these statements are simple, broad, overarching concepts that give a general feel about our program without getting into specifics of daily operations.

CNC's Nature Preschool Mission:
The mission of Nature Preschool is to provide a premier early childhood environment which meets the developmental needs of the whole child, while initiating them into a lifelong, meaningful relationship with the natural world.

CNC's Nature Preschool Philosophy:
At Nature Preschool we believe that children are intrinsically motivated to learn. The teaching staff promotes learning by:

- Providing an environment which encourages discovery, experimentation, and the opportunity to see the results of one's actions.
- Developing activities that encourage growth based on children's abilities and interests.
- Encouraging problem-solving and reflection by asking open-ended questions and providing information in response to children's ideas, insights, and concerns.
- Assisting children in their interactions with each other and offering opportunities for cooperative learning.
- Appreciating the individuality and diversity of children and families.

As you develop your nature preschool you'll be making hundreds of decisions related to your program. Every one of those decisions will help create the overall feel and experience you provide the children. Having a written statement to guide everyone involved helps give a clear direction during a very chaotic time in the life of your new preschool program. For example, CNC's philosophy statement about diversity led us to establish a scholarship program to ensure that we serve families of all socio-economic levels. This same statement means we don't celebrate religious or commercial holidays because we recognize that all families have their own traditions and beliefs, and there is no way we could be true to every one of those beliefs.

While these statements are primarily used to guide the growth and development of our program they are also helpful for parents to understand what our program is really about and whether it's a good fit for their family. By the way, in Michigan we're also required by child care licensing regulations to have these statements. The odds are good your state will require them too, so why not get a head start and write them now?

Finding a Location

Another question you should start asking very early in the process of developing your new program is, "Where will we house the preschool?" You really have two options: 1) use an existing facility or 2) build a new facility. At CNC we used an existing building for two years to determine if the program would be successful before investing in new construction. Once the program had proven itself we decided to build a new facility as part of our visitor center renovation project. No matter which route you take, be sure to acquire a copy of your state's child care licensing regulations. Licensing will be addressed more in the next chapter, but it's critical in determining if a space will work or not. For example, you'll want to know the minimum square footage requirements needed per child. Will the space you're considering accommodate your class size?

If you're retrofitting an existing space, there will probably be many small changes you'll need to make. Are the sinks and toilets at appropriate heights for the children? Are there enough restroom facilities for the children? Where will you store and prepare snacks and meals? Is this existing facility easy for parents to access? Is there enough parking? If you're using an existing space be prepared to make some sacrifices. The space may not be absolutely ideal, but the most vital thing is that it be a safe, comfortable learning environment for the children.

If you choose to build a new building for your preschool program let me first say, "Congratulations!" Building a space specifically for preschool children is very exciting and will make your program run even more smoothly. I could write an entire chapter, maybe even another book, on things to do and not do when building a new preschool building, but instead I'll focus on a few big items.

You're building a "nature" preschool, so being as green as possible makes good sense. Remember that you're creating a preschool very different from a traditional one, so it should look and feel different in the classroom. Maximize on the natural daylight coming into the classroom. Take advantage of views to nature—including low windows so the children can enjoy the view. Also be aware of typical design elements that may not be appropriate for preschool such as automatic flush toilets and sinks. These can be scary things for children, particularly the toilets, and don't teach children how to flush for themselves. Kitchens, dishwashers, washing machines, and built-in plumbing for the sand and water table are all important elements to include if you're building new. As you're designing, constantly ask yourself what would be ideal in a preschool classroom as a teacher and as a child. One more thing—do you think you have enough storage space planned? Add more. Trust me.

Another factor to consider in deciding where to house the program is the availability of the space during the summer. Preschool generally runs during the school year. However, there are opportunities for preschool-aged summer camps. Perhaps you'd like to conduct trainings for other preschool teachers on teaching in the outdoors. Does the space you're considering allow for these kinds of opportunities?

Yet another, and very important, factor in selecting a location is the outdoor play area. Ideally the play area will be accessible directly from the classroom. You'll need a space that will be large enough for the entire class, free of safety hazards, and as natural as possible—*natural* meaning there is dirt to dig in, trees to find shade under, sticks to build with, and so forth. There should be lots of natural "loose parts" for creative open-ended play. Depending on your state's licensing laws you may have to get a written variance for materials like sticks and rocks. Some states see these as safety hazards. When I say *safety hazards,* I mean things like dead tree snags, poison ivy, close proximity to parking lots and driveways, hidden areas out of the view of a teacher, etc.

The plethora of details to consider in the classroom and outdoor play area will be covered in Chapter 5. For now you don't need to work out every detail of your indoor and outdoor spaces. You just need to know that these spaces can be adapted to meet your state's licensing requirements and to meet the vision you have for your program. You also need to have an idea how much these improvements will cost and when they can be completed.

Selecting a Program Model

There are many choices related to the logistical details of your program. Every nature-based preschool uses a slightly different model. The early planning stage is the time to select what works for you and your community. You'll need to select the ages of children you'll serve, when to serve them, your staffing needs, what curriculum you'll use, and how the program will be funded. Let's talk a little more about each one of these areas.

Ages

Preschool is generally offered to three- to five-year-olds. That being said, some offer programs for two-year-olds as well and some don't offer a program for five-year-olds to encourage children to go on to kindergarten. At CNC we offer programs to three- and four-year olds who are potty-trained (an issue with a two-year-old program, for sure). When you determine the ages, you'll also need to determine a date that marks whether they're age eligible. The state's kindergarten cutoff date is an ideal option, as it fits with what parents will use to determine when their child goes on to kindergarten. In Michigan, this is December 1. So, they can start at two in September so long as they'll be three by December of that year. If they're five on December 1, they are eligible for kindergarten and we encourage them to pursue that.

Since I've brought up kindergarten, I should mention that kindergarten readiness is a very complicated, sensitive topic that varies from state to state and community to community. Ask your local preschool contact to give you some insights into this. Your community may have a developmental kindergarten or a "young fives" program. Essentially, this is intended to be an experience more in line with kindergarten for those children who are felt to "not be ready" for kindergarten. Hopefully your state or community has a clear definition of what it means to be "ready for kindergarten."

Curriculum

Selecting a curriculum model is pivotal in the overall direction and framework of your particular program. Early childhood curricula should provide direction on preparing the physical learning environment, developing a daily schedule of activities, and guiding the teacher/student interactions—not day-to-day instruction guides on what to teach. Many nature-based preschools have chosen to develop their own curriculum using elements of well-known curriculum models to allow them to meet all of their goals within the nature-based preschool concept. Personally, I don't believe a formal curriculum limits your ability to achieve your nature-based goals. Actually, I think selecting a formal curriculum model is a really strong move for any preschool, including a nature-based one, particularly because selecting a research-based curriculum adds to your credibility among the school community. Additionally, if you're receiving funds from your state to operate you will most likely have to select a model from a list of approved curricula.

Quality curriculum models share several key characteristics. They are based in research on the education and development of young children. They have also gone through extensive testing and research to ensure that there are positive child outcomes. They will have teacher resources and professional development trainings on implementing the curriculum so that all of the teachers will be speaking the same language. A quality curriculum should also have a standard system for student assessment. Using a well-established curriculum helps to ensure that all staff members are consistently implementing your overall philosophy.

If you decide to select a formal curriculum model, the next question is which one? A few of the many preschool curriculum models include: Bank Street, Curiosity Corner,® Creative Curriculum,® The Empowered Child,™ High/Scope, Montessori, The Project Approach, Reggio Emilia, and Tools of the Mind. Given the seasonal, discovery-based approach inherent in nature-based preschools, some models may be easier to implement than others—Creative Curriculum® and Reggio Emilia are at the top of this list. At CNC we chose to use Creative Curriculum.® I suggest researching which curriculum models your state department of education recommends or endorses.

There were two primary reasons we chose Creative Curriculum®: 1) We felt it would work nicely with our program philosophy and 2) Many of the preschools in our county, including Head Start and all of the state-funded programs, use this model—allowing for more training opportunities and better communications with kindergarten teachers, for example. Creative Curriculum® focuses on preparing the learning environment with 11 different interest areas, such as library, dramatic play, and outdoors. This model also helps teachers to adapt the environment to meet the varying developmental levels within the class. Creative Curriculum® encourages teachers to help extend children's learning interests through studies. Parent involvement is another component of this curriculum model that fits nicely with our overall program philosophy.

Early childhood professionals who visit our program will often comment on the similarities between our program and Reggio Emilia—another great curriculum choice for a nature-based preschool. This model, named for the Italian city where it originated, involves teachers, students, and parents in the educational process where studies emerge as the result of the children's interests. Teachers are discovering and learning along with the children. The physical environment, with lots of natural elements, is also an important part of a Reggio Emilia class—branches and bird mounts hanging in the classroom for example. The learning process is highly individualized, which is core to this preschool philosophy.

A quality curriculum should also have a standard system for student assessment. These assessments should be developmentally appropriate and address all developmental domains. Teaching Strategies Gold® uses observations of children's behaviors and knowledge, which are recorded by the teachers, as the primary assessment tool. Reggio Emilia typically uses a portfolio assessment system where children's works are used to assess learning. No matter how it's done, the goal of assessment should be to support individual children's learning and development, and determine where children could use more support. Good assessment is also valuable in communicating with parents about their child's progress. As with a curriculum, the assessment tool should be research-based, not self-developed.

As you can see, there are many things to consider when selecting a curriculum. Ideally your program director and/or lead teacher will be part of the selection of your curriculum model. You're hiring early childhood experts and this is a prime example of where their expertise is needed. In the end, whether you develop your own or choose a formal curriculum, be sure your staff fully understands the philosophy and guidelines they are to follow. Consistency among all of your staff is crucial to individual child success, which leads to overall program success.

Timing

There are several elements of "timing." You'll need to select a length of time for the class period, how often and when that class meets each week, the beginning and ending dates for the school year, and which days are holidays.

The length of your day will be driven by your curriculum and what is included in the daily schedule. For example, when we first started our program, it was two and a half hours long. However, we found we weren't getting a full hour of indoor choice time because we were spending so much of the day outside. We didn't want to cut into our outside time and yet we recognized that children need extended free choice time, so we chose to extend the program to three hours.

Determining how often and what days of the week a class meets is a more complicated decision. Having classes that meet more often, say four days per week, will mean you are able to serve fewer children. However, it also means in the first couple of years that you'll need to enroll fewer children to reach capacity. You can also adjust the number of days in a program to allow for a class to be one age versus mixed ages. When we first started our program we offered a four-day-per-week, half-day class in the morning and afternoon. In 2010–11 we offered a full-day class (Monday through Thursday) for four-year-olds only; a half-day class (Monday, Wednesday, and Friday) for three- and four-year-olds; a half-day class (Tuesday and Thursday) for three-year-olds only; and a half-day class (Monday through Thursday) for three- and four-year-olds. Keep in mind a full-day session requires two snacks, lunch, rest time, and other unique licensing requirements. You also have to work in breaks for the teaching staff.

Our most popular sessions are by far the morning half-day sessions. The afternoon session has always been the last to fill—a trend among most preschools due primarily to napping schedules. In 2011–12, we eliminated the full-day class and offered two half-day sessions in its place based on demand. This illustrates the importance of adjusting to the needs of the families you're serving.

The beginning and ending dates of your program and holiday schedule are probably the easiest timing questions to answer. We select a beginning date about a week after the public schools open and end a week or two before they close for the year. This is typical throughout our community. As for holidays, we follow our local school district's calendar. This allows for the preschool child to have the same vacations as an older sibling, hopefully making life easier on our families. We also follow the local school district for any school closures that may occur during the year, such as snow days and fog delays. By doing this, we don't have to make any early-morning decisions or calls to families. They know if school is closed so is preschool.

Staff

Most preschool directors would agree that the most critical element of your program's success is the staff. In Chapter 4 we'll talk more about the hiring process and specific needs of staff. For now it's time to think about how many people and in what positions you'll need to make your program successful. Programs that are well established and serve multiple classrooms tend to have the following staff:

1. Program director (who may or may not have teaching duties)
2. Administrative assistant
3. Cook (if serving meals in a full day class)
4. Lead teacher (Some programs use a co-teacher model rather than having a lead and assistants.)
5. Assistant teacher(s)
6. Support staff (maintenance, housekeeping)
7. Early childhood specialist (a consultant and integral part of the team)

When first starting out, you may not be able to hire all of these positions. When we started, we hired the teaching staff only. We weren't serving meals, so we didn't need a cook. Administrative and clerical duties were and still are being handled by the director of education. Classroom cleaning is done by our existing maintenance staff. Now that the program has grown by an additional classroom and we're serving meals we've added teaching staff and a cook. As we near capacity and are beginning to earn a profit we're looking at adding an administrative assistant to handle the clerical responsibilities.

Funding Children

There are many options when it comes to how children enrollment is funded—tuition-based, tuition on a sliding scale, scholarships, cooperative programs, grant-funded, etc. A driving force in this decision is your overall organizational/program philosophy and mission. How much profit are you looking to make? Are you trying to reach all socio-economic groups in your community? Another factor is your community—what is the current standard? What will the community support?

Let's talk a bit about what the different payment models mean. Tuition-based, the most straightforward model, is where families pay one price for the services you provide. Tuition on a sliding scale means your definition of "full price" changes based on the income level of the family. A scholarship program essentially means you'll charge families less due to their income level, but will make up the difference between their payment and full tuition through a scholarship fund. A cooperative preschool typically charges tuition, but parents have a reduced tuition for working a defined number of hours in the classroom.

There are also grant-funded models. Some states, such as Michigan, have grants available to school and nonprofits for serving at-risk children. You may also be able to secure a grant from a private foundation, or some other granting source, that would allow you to provide tuition on a sliding scale. Or perhaps you could secure an individual donor contribution to an endowed scholarship fund. The possibilities here really are endless.

There are a wide variety of possibilities for funding the children. At CNC our children are funded one of three ways. We have full tuition, scholarships based on family income, and a grant through the state of Michigan to serve at-risk children called the Great Start Readiness Program. This grant is a result of our partnership with the West Midland Family Center, a local nonprofit that serves families in our community and serves as the fiduciary for the state grant. About 60 percent of the children in our program pay full tuition where the other 40 percent receive some level of assistance to help offset their tuition costs.

As you can see, there are lots of possible combinations of program offerings. Choose what makes sense for your organization and your community's needs and it will be the best combination. And worst-case scenario—if something doesn't work this year, you can change it next year.

4

Administrative Needs Before the Kids Arrive

Most educators, whether formal or informal, love spending time establishing the classroom and developing new activity ideas. When creating a nature-based preschool, however, there are many administrative needs to tend to long before the programming fun can begin. In this chapter I'll address the various administrative needs you'll face head-on. No doubt there is a lot to think about, but it is all quite manageable.

Licensing

One of the first things you'll want to do, perhaps even before you make a final decision about pursuing a nature-based preschool, is to get a copy of your state's childcare licensing guidelines for child care centers. Which department regulates childcare centers differs from state to state. In Michigan, the oversight comes from the Department of Human Services. Michigan also has a "technical assistance" document, which accompanies the licensing rules and gives explanations of the rules and suggestions for how to implement those rules. Many states also offer training days to better understand the rules.

You'll be referencing this licensing document daily—and long after the doors of your preschool have opened. The licensing rules will guide how many staff you hire and their qualifications, how many children you can register for each class, what building modifications you need to make, what items are included in your policy manual, and more. You will need to begin working on complying with the licensing regulations months in advance. A prime example of taking steps to comply with licensing in advance is the inspection process.

As part of licensing, and prior to being able to open, you'll receive one or more

HOLLY MAHAFFEY

Quality teachers create the overall atmosphere of any preschool program.

inspections. When you first receive the licensing documents determine what inspections will be required within the licensing process. Do not be casual in your preparation for these. Many of these inspections have costs associated with them, and knowing the requirements in advance will help with generating an accurate budget. Also keep an eye out for inspections within inspections. For example, in Michigan, we're required to have an environmental health inspection. If you read the rules a little more closely there is also a requirement for a lead inspection (i.e., chipping paint) if your building was built before a certain date. This inspection must be done prior to the environmental health inspection, both of which must be completed before receiving a license. Many inspections also take time to schedule—after all, you're not the only program inspectors are visiting. Early awareness of the timing and cost of inspections will reduce your headaches in the long run.

My advice on licensing is simple: Get the rule book early and learn it like the back of your hand. You won't regret it.

Policy Manual

A written policy manual is a licensing requirement and many of the specific elements within the manual are also requirements. Remember, a policy manual is not supposed to be a great literary work—just the primary elements your staff need to know to keep everyone in the program safe. Keep it clear, simple, and easy to understand. Every preschool you've visited in your planning process has a policy manual. I highly recommend using those as a starting point. Particularly take note of manuals for programs in your state as they'll be following the same licensing rules as your program.

Once again, be sure to check the licensing requirements as you go. Most all of your policies will come from the licensing rules. There will be a few policies that you'll need to include specific to a nature-based preschool, such as group management on the trail, pond hazards, etc. General policy topics include:

- Screening policy for staff and volunteers
- Employee code of ethics
- Staff records and training plan
- Management of children's records
- Emergency procedures (building evacuation, serious accident or injury, missing student, armed subject)
- Signs of child abuse and procedures for reporting suspected abuse
- Health care plan (dealing with a sick child, cleaning schedule, etc.)
- Snow days and other school closings
- Procedures for field trips
- Basic program overview and philosophy
- Discipline and classroom behavior management
- Communication with families

Policies specific to a nature-based preschool may include:

- Group management outside of the play area (on hikes, around ponds, etc.)
- Addressing hazards in play area (dead snags, poison ivy, etc.)

- Animals in the classroom
- Animals outside the classroom

A well written, concise, and easy-to-understand policy manual will ensure that your staff is implementing your program philosophy in a safe and responsible way.

Staffing

It can't be emphasized enough that selecting the right staff for your program will be the most important decision you can make to ensure your program is successful. It's the people in your program who will make the connections with the children and parents, who will bring the creativity and passion to lesson plans, and who will create the overall atmosphere of the program.

After you've determined what positions you'll need comes the hard part—finding the perfect person for each of those positions. Be sure to start this process well ahead of your first day of school—several months is ideal. This is for two primary reasons: 1) You'll want the staff to be part of the planning and set-up process, and 2) There is a great deal of paperwork to complete for licensing that takes time and can't be completed overnight.

If you're hiring a director, that will be the first and most significant hire you'll make. After that, your emphasis should be on the teaching staff. I recommend hiring the lead teacher first and then having that person participate in hiring the assistant teachers. Minimum qualifications for the teaching positions will be determined by licensing and/or your state's pre-K standards. Qualifications beyond that are up to you. Ideally a nature-based preschool teacher has both early childhood and environmental education experience. Unfortunately these people are hard to come by. As a program you have to decide what is most valuable to you, but generally the emphasis for the lead teacher should be on early childhood education. Every teaching team is different in its exact make up, but all should be the same overall—a blend of early childhood and outdoor education. No matter the backgrounds of your staff, you always want all of your teachers to have a passion for getting children outside. They don't necessarily need to have professional outdoor or environmental experience, but they must believe in your program's mission and philosophy. For example, outdoor-based hobbies show that a candidate has an interest in your program philosophy.

The interview process is critical in finding people who have received quality training and have strong preschool experience, and who also have a passion for connecting children to nature. If at all possible you should see these candidates, at minimum the

ᑭEWA NATURE CENTER

Staff should have quality training, strong preschool experience, and a passion for connecting children to nature.

lead teacher, actually working with preschool-aged children. If preschool children aren't available, get children as close to that age as possible. It's important to make sure the staff can relate to preschool children and that they know what activities and language is developmentally appropriate. When we hired our first lead teacher at CNC, we conducted a traditional question-and-answer interview with five candidates. From there we narrowed the pool to three candidates. We then had these final candidates teach a 10- to 15-minute lesson with three different groups of preschool children. Our local family center agreed to bring a group of preschool children to the nature center for this half-day experience. The children were divided into three groups and experienced each of the three teachers' mini-lessons. Our search committee observed each of the candidates and received feedback from the family center teachers.

In addition to the question-and-answer and teaching interviews, we had the lead teacher candidates complete a written assignment. This assignment had two parts. The first was to write a letter introducing themselves and their teaching philosophy to the parents. This is good insight into this candidate's skills in communicating with parents, a critical skill for the lead teacher to have. The second part of the assignment was to generate a list of materials they would include in three of the different interest areas within the classroom to make that area more "nature-based." This might seem like a very simple task, but we were surprised at how it clearly distinguished those candidates who really understood and embraced our program philosophy.

In a perfect world, hiring assistant teachers would follow this same format. Unfortunately, you'll probably find yourself crunched for time. So at the very least you'll want to conduct a face-to-face interview with the candidates to discuss their early childhood and outdoor experience. Again, I encourage you to hire your lead teacher first and then have that person involved in the hiring of assistants. This will help ensure a cohesive team, which will pay huge dividends in the future.

As you're interviewing, keep in mind that you'll soon need to have a pool of quality substitute teachers. Are any of the candidates you didn't hire potential substitutes? Whether it's regular staff or substitute staff, hiring the right people is absolutely critical. The atmosphere in any preschool building hinges on the attitudes and skills of the staff. Don't rush the interviewing process and you're sure to be on your way to a successful program!

State and Federal Programs

Be sure to familiarize yourself with any state and federal programs that might benefit your program. These may be programs that help with tuition—such as a grant program for at-risk kids or childcare payments through the state. It could also be a program reimbursing portions of snacks and meals such as the one through the U.S. Department of Agriculture. (Oversight and implementation of this food program varies from state to state.) The best way to find out about these programs is to ask other preschool experts in your community such as local school districts are Head Start providers. Many of these programs have application processes and extensive paperwork, so learning about them early is necessary if you're going to implement them in your inaugural year.

Publicity and Marketing

While you're in the process of hiring staff, getting the building set up, and ordering furniture…you'll also need to start registering students. Yikes! The first class of students is probably the biggest challenge you'll face, so publicity and marketing is crucial. You'll need to begin this process early, as many parents begin enrolling their children as early as January for the fall session. Remember that many parents will do extensive research before selecting a preschool. In general, even with researching programs, parents select a preschool based on word of mouth. If their friends, neighbors, or coworkers sent a child to the program and enjoyed it, they're more likely to send their own child. Unfortunately, in the first year, you won't have that word of mouth. However, if you're an existing organization, you do have word of mouth about the quality of your other programming (school programs, scout groups, day camp, etc.), which will be very helpful and the primary source for your first class of students.

For the most part, this word-of-mouth publicity is out of your control. Let's address the things you can control in the first year or two regarding publicity and marketing. First, start with the marketing methods you already use on a regular basis. If you're an existing nature center you probably have a membership or friends group. These people are already your supporters and believe in the work you do. Make sure they know about the new program—both the value and the logistical details. If you have a regular mailed newsletter and/or electronic newsletter, make sure the preschool is mentioned as often as possible. If you distribute a summer camp brochure or any other marketing specific to youth programming be sure you include information about the preschool. Even before you know the registration details, include "coming soon" teasers to build community interest.

As we all know, electronic marketing methods abound. I mentioned the electronic newsletter already. Make sure your organization's website has information about the program listed as soon as possible. Again, you don't need to have all the details yet, but you do need to start building interest as soon as possible. Facebook, Twitter, and other social networking sites are another great opportunity for spreading the word. After all, preschool parents are the right demographic to be active users of these social network sites.

Outside of electronic promotion, you'll want to pursue some traditional marketing methods as well. Contact your local newspaper (if you're still fortunate enough to have one!) and ask them about any regular sections they have on children's activities or preschools. While you have them on the phone why not mention the unique program you're establishing and see if they'd like to do a story on the program? We had great luck with our local newspapers wanting to cover this new program. Remember, they're looking for unique and different news stories and in most towns a nature-based preschool is just the ticket. The other method we had good success with was hanging posters around town. We put them in windows at restaurants, party stores (Michigan's name for convenience stores), laundromats, coffee shops, and children's clothing stores. However, by far the most successful location was the local library.

As soon as your facility is ready and you've hired at least one teacher, you'll want to begin hosting open houses. I mentioned that word of mouth is the most effective marketing tool and one of the biggest factors in a parent's decision about preschool. The second biggest factor tends to be experiencing the program in person. The factors that make or break the experience are the staff and the facility. At CNC we now host three or four open houses around the time of registration and any time we are hosting a major event at the nature center (e.g., Fall Festival, Maple Syrup Day). The more opportunities people have to see your facility and meet the staff the better. By the way, this includes local school officials such as superintendents and principals. If they have a strong understanding of your program they're more likely to refer families.

The wonderful thing about a nature-based preschool is that if you focus on having a quality program, soon the marketing will take on a life of its own. The effort we put into marketing our first year was significantly more than the effort (and money!) we put into our fourth year. That is, without a doubt, because of the power of parents talking with each other. By the way, you'll also start filling spots with younger siblings of alumni, which means fewer new families you need to find. Until this starts to happen, promote your program any way you can—the more people who know about it the better. We all have family, friends, neighbors, and coworkers, and someone is bound to need a good preschool.

Registration

You'll know you're really starting a preschool when you actually start registering children! Up to this point, it's just been a concept, but now it's real. Very real. Parents have many questions when it comes to registering their child for preschool. The best approach is to have a packet of information that accompanies the actual registration form. At the very least, your registration booklet should include the following information:

- Mission
- Philosophy
- Curriculum used and a basic overview of that curriculum
- Schedule of class offerings
- School year start and end dates (if you follow a particular school district's schedule for holidays and school closures, mention it here)
- Facility information (number of classrooms, size, location, etc.)
- Enrollment policy and procedures
- Payment schedule for tuition

- Scholarship information (if applicable)
- Expectations of parent involvement
- Explanation of how snacks and meals are handled and the kinds of items you serve (if applicable)
- Registration form
- Scholarship form (if applicable)
- Dates of upcoming open houses
- Enrollment dates
- Contact information in case they have questions

It's also a nice touch to include a note to the parents thanking them for their interest, giving them a brief explanation of your program, and offering your contact information if they have any questions. This adds a personal touch, which helps create the family atmosphere that is so important in a successful preschool.

There may be some parents who want a few more details on the program. More than likely, you'll include answers to those questions in the parent handbook. Thus, it's ideal to create the parent handbook about the same time as the registration booklet, so both documents are available to parents. We'll talk more about the parent handbook shortly.

When to release this registration booklet depends on your particular community. In many communities registration for the fall begins as early as January. As a result, we typically publish the registration booklet for the next school year at the end of December or beginning of January. When it comes to actual registration, we allow current and alumni families to register first. We give them two weeks to register before opening registration to the general public. This encourages families to register early to insure they get their preferred class session. A small registration fee along with the registration form is common in most communities. This non-refundable fee helps discourage families from registering at multiple schools before making a final decision.

After we receive a child's registration we place children in their preferred class sessions, ideally their first choice, and send a written confirmation. This confirmation lists the class session they've been placed in, the start dates of school, and when they'll be receiving the next communication. With this written confirmation we also send a copy of the parent handbook and a storybook for the child. We wait to send out the full enrollment packet (emergency contact forms, health forms, etc.) until about two months before the start of school.

Once registration begins it's a matter of wait and see. It's interesting from year to year to see which sessions fill first and which are a little slower to fill. You can count on the morning sessions filling first. Beyond that, it's hard to predict. You can also anticipate having a flurry of registrations right when you open enrollment. After that, it will be slow but steady. Don't panic if you're not full in the first month of registration. Preschool is a big decision for families. It's also not something many families think about until closer to the start of the school year—particularly families who haven't had a school-aged child yet. Be patient. The students will come. Just keep up on your marketing and you'll be fine. Also, be realistic in your expectations—filling to capacity in your first year isn't always realistic. This can be a blessing in disguise, because it allows your staff to work out the kinks of the program before managing a full class load.

Parent Handbook

Another document you'll need to create is a parent handbook. This document is useful for some families when they're in the process of selecting a preschool. It's also a resource document for parents throughout the school year. It should give them all of the information they need to know before and during their child's time in your preschool. We send the parent handbook with the registration confirmation and distribute another copy during parent orientation. We also have copies available in the family waiting area in our building and have it posted on our website. When creating your parent handbook be sure to include:

- Contact information for the school and teachers
- Names and titles of preschool staff
- Mission
- Program philosophy
- Curriculum (this should be more detailed than in the registration booklet)
- Sample schedule of a typical day
- School year start and end dates
- Holidays and school closures (days off as well as how you handle celebrations in the classroom)

- Explanation of how snacks and meals are handled and the kinds of items you serve (include your procedures for bringing birthday snacks to class)
- Clothing suggestions (provide a list for each season of the school year)
- Expectations for parent involvement
- Registration requirements (health forms, immunizations, copy of birth certificate, etc.)
- Enrollment policy
- Payment schedule for tuition
- Scholarship information (if applicable)
- Withdrawal policy
- Behavior expectations for the children
- Discipline policy and philosophy
- Field trip procedures
- Attendance related to child illness

Be sure to check the licensing rules for your state for any other items you may need to include. For example, we also include an explanation of the screening process any of our volunteers must go through before being in the classroom. We are also required to include our health care plan in the parent handbook. This includes when and how we clean the classroom, our procedures for dealing with a sick child, etc. As time goes on, you may find there are other items that should be included in your parent handbook. Include anything that helps make preschool an easier experience for the families.

5

Program Needs—The Kids Are on Their Way!

Okay, it's finally here. The chapter you've been waiting for—the programming chapter! Now that you've gone through all of the logistical blood, sweat, and tears you can finally focus on the best part of this entire preschool development process (short of the kids arriving, of course). It's time to develop the program itself! Now is when you determine what the layout of the indoor classroom will be, the outdoor play area layout, the materials you'll need for both the indoor and outdoor spaces, your daily program schedule, and how you'll communicate with the families. This is when everything comes together and the facility starts to feel and look like the preschool you've been dreaming of for so long. Plus, and I guess I just might as well go ahead and say it—this is *really* the best part of the process because it's when you get to buy the fun toys, books, equipment, and furniture!

Child-height window sills blur the lines between indoor and outdoor spaces.

Preparing the Indoor Space

As much as we'd like to be outside the entire school day, the fact is, indoor time is necessary. The preschool environment should support learning and encourage creative play, and bring the outside in as much as possible. Different curricula have different terms and requirements for the areas within a classroom, but you'll notice that, no matter what they're called, the elements are similar from curriculum to curriculum. At CNC, we use the Creative Curriculum,® which calls the learning areas "interest areas." The Creative Curriculum® interest areas include:

- Library
- Blocks
- Dramatic play
- Discovery
- Art
- Sand and water
- Music and movement
- Toys and games
- Cooking
- Computers (technology)*
- Outdoors

Class pets are an important part of nature-based preschool. Here Ansel Adams, CNC's class rabbit, poses for the camera.

*It will be hard to find a curriculum that matches your program philosophy perfectly. At Nature Preschool we have chosen not to include the "Computer" interest area. We feel children are already exposed to an excessive amount of screen time in their daily lives and do not need more at preschool. We do, however, explore technology in other ways. As you move forward with your planning don't be afraid to incorporate your own program philosophy.

Any preschool classroom in the country will have most of the elements listed above, though they may have different names and the materials provided will vary. The difference with a nature-based preschool is that each of these areas will have nature infused into them. For example, in the library area the books should include children's books with a nature focus, and you should also include things like field guides (e.g., birds, tracks) and science reference books. In the music area we have the obligatory guitar and maracas, but we also include rain sticks, turkey calls, and squirrel calls. The block area has tree blocks in addition to traditional ones. Collections of rocks, pinecones, shells, feathers, and seeds are in our discovery area. Throughout the classroom we have furs, skulls, and other bones. Be creative and constantly ask the question, "How can we bring the outdoors inside?" See Appendix B for sources for toys and equipment and Appendix C for a list of some must-have children's books.

There are other things beyond these play areas to consider when planning your indoor space. A few of these considerations for your indoor space include:

- Will you have a class pet? If so, where will the pet live? Where will its supplies be kept?
- Storage of extra clothes (i.e., base layers for each child such as socks and underwear; and outer layers for children that may forget an item)
- Space for parents and children to sign-in each day
- Parent "mailboxes" for sending written communication home to families
- Children's cubbies for storing coats, indoor shoes, etc.
- Individual staff gear storage (for their outdoor gear and indoor shoes)

Preparing the Outdoor Play Area

The outdoor play area(s) should be seen as an extension of your classroom. (In fact, it should be the other way around—the indoor classroom should be seen as an extension of your outdoor play area—but that's semantics.) The outdoor play area is a safe and secure area, almost always fenced, where the children can explore, build, create, and discover at their own pace and of their own choosing. Like any aspect of a quality preschool, the environment should support the child's learning. That means including quality elements that will encourage learning through creative play.

HOLLY MAHAFFEY

Loose parts such as sticks, logs, leaves, rocks, buckets, and shovels allow for open-ended play.

Now, please repeat after me: "Loose parts, loose parts, loose parts." Thank you for your participation. I asked you to do that because it can't be said enough that the outdoor play area should be loaded with loose parts. "Loose parts" is a term coined by Simon Nicholson, a landscape architect, to refer to items that can be manipulated and have endless possibilities for play—they're open-ended. The outdoor play area should include natural loose parts like logs, leaves, rocks, and water, but should also include human-made loose parts like buckets, shovels, spoons, tarps, and wagons. Here are a few suggestions for loose parts to include in your play area:

- Logs
- Tree cookies
- Stumps
- Rocks (all sizes)
- Dirt piles

HOLLY MAHAFFEY

The outdoor play area is ever-changing with the help of quality teachers.

- Sand
- Spoons
- Shovels
- Wheelbarrows
- Tricycles—with and without trailers
- Wagons
- Dump trucks
- Wide array of sand toys
- Water! (which also means a need for watering cans, squirt bottles, colanders…)

In addition to these loose parts it's important to have a few formal structures. A nature-based play area looks very different from a traditional one, and the play structures are probably the most glaring difference. Generally, a natural play area doesn't include traditional elements like swings and plastic climbing structures. The structures you'll find in a natural area tend to be made of wood and provide opportunities for open-ended learning, much like the loose parts. The structures also expand on the theme of outdoor adventures and experiences. There are endless possibilities for "structures" or permanent fixtures within a natural play area. A few of those include:

- Miniature log cabin
- Oversized sand box with logs marking the boundaries
- Stage—with or without a roof
- Wooden canoe or row boat
- Acrylic easel for outdoor painting projects (moveable or mounted to the fence)
- Tricycle track (a surface that is hard-packed enough for riding)
- Kid-sized picnic tables
- Talk tubes (where children talk through either end of a pipe)
- Crawling tunnels (concrete, hollow logs, or other materials)
- Good climbing tree
- Weaving frame (wooden frame with monofilament tied into a grid pattern)
- Water feature (re-circulating miniature creek, rain barrels, kid-size fountain, etc.)
- Creative storage for all of your loose parts

CHIPPEWA NATURE CENTER

In the winter one of the group excursions at CNC is focused on animal rescue. Here the students are practicing check, call, care as they "rescue" the stuffed animal.

Again, the possibilities are endless for the outdoor play area structures. The trick is to have a variety of structures that will help encourage diverse and creative play. Keep in mind that the play area should help create a sense of place by reflecting your community. In other words, rely on the natural and cultural features that exist in your community. Maybe you live by a large river with huge bridges, barges, and tug boats. The play area could then have a miniature tugboat with a pilothouse and a kid-sized captain's wheel. The beauty of a nature-based preschool is you're focusing on the natural features, which have naturally formed the cultural features of your community. In other words, you're maximizing children's learning by encouraging play that reflects their daily lives—which is essential to quality early-childhood education.

Of course, through it all, you should be referencing your childcare licensing rules. (Yup, you're starting to think like a preschool administrator, because you knew I was going to bring that up at some point in this chapter.) Your state may require an inspection of the play area. In some cases, because of the uniqueness of your play area, you may need to write a letter explaining how your play area is regularly inspected for any safety hazards.

Even with licensing considerations looming, designing the play area should be a fun and creative project. Visit as many natural play areas as you can, think about the play elements you loved as a kid, talk with playground designers and landscape architects, check out the resources in Appendix B—anything to get your creative mind working on play area ideas. Most importantly—have fun. It's a *play* area after all!

Daily Schedule

In Chapter 3, we discussed the length of time for your program. No matter what you choose, you'll want to be consistent in your schedule from day to day. As with the indoor areas, each curriculum will likely have different terms for the various elements, but generally the typical preschool day includes the same basic elements. At CNC's Nature Preschool a typical day is reflected on the chart on pages 66 and 67.

Many of these daily components will be seen in traditional preschool classrooms as well. What distinguishes a nature-based preschool is the activities within these daily components. Let the seasons and what's happening in the natural world guide your weekly topics and day-to-day activities. The trick is to put a seasonal, outdoor twist on developmentally appropriate activities. This will include the hikes you take, songs you sing, and books you read. During maple syrup season, for example, the group excursions could be a hike to tap maple trees and collect sap. Then during large group time the students can count the buckets of sap collected and how much syrup that sap can make. Maple syrup season isn't a theme per se, but rather the daily activities align with the happenings at that time of the year.

For specific activity ideas by season, check out Dodge Nature Preschool's book *Four Seasons at a Nature Based Preschool.* While it focuses on activities related to seasonal changes in the Upper Midwest, anyone looking for nature-based activities for young children will find value in this book. Another activity resource is the Schlitz Audubon Nature Preschool's brain development cards, called *Naturally Developing Young Brains*, which give activity suggestions and the brain development those activities relate to. (See Appendix B for ordering information.)

Ultimately quality daily activities hinge on high-quality, creative, talented staff. If you hire the best possible staff to match your program philosophy, you'll not only have no concerns about the teachers coming up with great activities you'll be amazed daily by their creativity! Trust me—it happens to me every day.

ᴾPEWA NATURE CENTER

Children arrive to preschool dressed for the weather—whatever it is that particular day.

Parent Orientation

Parent orientation is designed to make parents feel comfortable about their child attending school. They are more nervous than they will ever tell you. After all, they're entrusting you with the child they love. So, your job is to make sure they have a clear understanding of what to expect once school starts. You may feel like you're overwhelming families with information, but there really are no details that are too small. We share information using a PowerPoint with lots of photos and information on the following:

- Overview of a typical day
- Review of the program philosophy and typical activities
- Clothing requirements for each season
- Sign-in/sign-out procedures for parents

DAILY SCHEDULE, CHIPPEWA NATURE CENTER

Outdoor Play

This is choice time for the children in the outdoor play areas. We start the day outside because the children are already dressed which reduces transitions throughout the day. Starting with outdoor play also places emphasis on the outdoor portion of the program—you're doing the most important thing first. This procedure of outdoor play first is also in keeping with research that indicates children are better able to focus after outdoor play, suggesting their indoor play is of higher quality after outdoor play.

Group Excursion

Each day the group leaves the boundaries of the play area to explore a natural feature in the area. The group will meet briefly before heading out to explain the purpose of the day's outing. This meeting might include a story, visit from a puppet, or some other activity to get the kids focused on the particular topic of the day. One day the excursion might be a visit to the pond in search of frogs and the next it might be a trip to the woods to make a pinecone collection. Some days it might not be directly related to a nature event at all—such as finding the missing letters of their names somewhere in the woods.

The hikes will increase in length as the year goes on. In fact, if a new student joins mid-year the teachers will often notice that child doesn't have the same endurance as the other students. Note: At CNC, we do not go on group excursions the first week of school. This gives teachers and students a chance to know each other and to build comfort and trust with one another. Instead we'll spend more time in the outdoor play area.

Large Group

At this time the whole class and all the teachers gather for a story, song, dance, etc. Generally the large group time will help connect back to the group excursion and help reinforce the learning related to that week's topic.

Snack

Teachers and students all sit down for snack, which is served family style. *Family style* means there are kid-sized pitchers of milk, juice, or water and bowls of whatever the snack is with serving utensils. Children serve themselves, pour their own drinks, and then pass the dishes on to the next student. Family-style snacks teach children lots of skills—knowing how soon to stop pouring into the glass before it overflows, taking care of your own needs including asking for what you need, patience while you wait for others to serve themselves, and basic table manners like *please* and *thank you*. Increasingly, families do not eat meals together. Snack is an opportunity for a shared meal experience. Once children are finished eating they may excuse themselves, clean up their place, and begin choice time in the classroom. By doing this, we acknowledge the time for snack and conversation together, but it also allows the children who are done eating to move on to the next activity at their own pace.

Indoor Choice Time

This is time for child-directed play in the classroom. Children are free to move from interest area to interest area as they wish. It's important that this be a significant chunk of uninterrupted time for them to play—an hour is ideal. During this time teachers will be busy helping the children to identify and resolve any problems they might be having, but also to engage in and extend the play that's happening in the classroom through sharing and collaboration.

Small Group

Each teacher meets with a group of five to six children to focus on a particular activity or skill. This time is very short, but allows for focused skill development and assessment. Activities might focus on sorting, writing, or an art project and will have a nature-based slant as often as possible. For example, on wet spring days a small group might focus on sorting worms based on length. The focus of the activity isn't the worm, but it's much more fun to determine the length of a squirmy worm than a line on a piece of paper.

- Snack procedures
- What to bring and what to expect on the first day
- Tuition payment procedures
- Parent volunteering expectations and sign-up for first two months
- Overview of parent communication throughout the year
- Overview of and sign-up for home visits

Be sure to have written information for parents to take home with them such as another copy of the parent handbook. We also distribute a written copy of the packing list for the first day of school, a copy of the school year calendar, and information about our curriculum. Again, the goal is for parents to feel fully prepared for the first day of school.

Meeting the Kids Before the First Day

The first day of preschool is stressful—for everyone. Teachers are stressed about setting the right tone on the first day. Parents are worried about their babies growing up and going to their first day of school. Students are scared about starting something new and unknown. However, there are things you can do to reduce everyone's anxiety. Ideally there will be at least two opportunities for students and parents to meet the teachers prior to the first day of school. At CNC we offer an open house for enrolled families and conduct a visit to each student's home.

Our August open house is held a day or two after parent orientation. We encourage parents to go home after orientation and "talk up" the great things they saw and the teachers they met. Then parents bring the child back for an open house to meet the teachers, explore the classroom, find their cubbies, and so forth. This visit helps students understand what is going to happen when they go to school for the first day. It also starts building a relationship with one or more of the teachers.

Between the open house and the first day of school, the teachers will make visits to each student's home. Two of the student's teachers will visit the home for 15 to 20 minutes. Children tend to warm up more quickly when they're in their own environment. They show off their room, favorite toys, introduce pets, etc. This visit is also a time for parents to ask any last-minute questions that haven't been answered or they haven't felt comfortable asking up to that point. Be mindful that for some families, particularly low-income families, this can be an intimidating event. During the visit, the teachers will also take a photo of the child with his or her family, which will be posted in the classroom for the child to see on the first day of school.

Then it's time for the first day of school! Yet another way we reduce the stress is to have half of the class attend on day one, the other half attend on day two, and then the entire class attends on day three. We make sure families are aware of their first day of school when we send enrollment materials. Some families will need to make child care arrangements, so it's helpful that they understand the schedule as soon as possible.

All of these activities are designed to reduce stress and ease the transition by creating trust among the teachers, students, and parents. By instituting these steps you'll be on your way to a smooth routine every day.

Parent Involvement Throughout the Year

A child's success in preschool depends on several things, but a major factor is the active involvement of his/her parent(s) in the preschool experience. This includes volunteering in the classroom, attending social gatherings for families, and taking advantage of materials sent home with the child. One of the signs of a quality preschool is the number of opportunities available for parent involvement.

Volunteering

At CNC parents are asked to volunteer at least once monthly. It's not a requirement, but highly encouraged. Grandparents and other relatives are welcome to volunteer as well. (For some families, this eases some stress due to work schedules.) Children love to share their classroom, introduce their teachers, and have a play day with their guest. Perhaps even more valuable is the benefit the parents receive. By volunteering parents see the teachers' styles and personalities, the lessons being taught, the expectations of the children, and the interactions the child is having with the other kids and teachers. Parents who are aware of the child's daily experiences are better prepared to help the child make connections between their in-school time and their out-of-school time.

Parent Education

There is no doubt that parent involvement is a key element to a child's success, and preschools have a responsibility to prepare parents as much as possible for contributing to that success. Many preschools have had success with trainings designed specifically for the parents. Topics might include behavior management, transitioning to kindergarten, or dealing with sibling conflicts. At CNC we have had minimal success with these nights. It's a lot to ask of parents to find a babysitter and attend a training—just one more thing on their list of things to do. Some preschools offer parent trainings during the school day. It all depends on your particular audience. Maybe there are opportunities for you to partner with local schools or family centers providing parent education. At minimum, make sure parents are always made aware of local resources and trainings. Also include articles in your monthly newsletter that gives parents knowledge and skills to support their child's education.

Family Nights

Family nights are fun evenings for the whole family to socialize with other preschool families. Picnics, dinners, potlucks, ice cream socials—anything that combines games and food is sure to be a success! Take advantage of the other facilities at your center, such as a farm area or visitor center. Be sure to have name tags for everyone, as classroom parents may not know each other and definitely won't know the names of parents from other classes. Ideally the first family night would be scheduled a month or so into school. This will help create more conversations and interactions among parents at pick-up and drop-off times throughout the school year. The goal is to connect families to each other through a fun, low-pressure social experience.

Family Literacy Packs

Family literacy packs are the closest thing to homework we give to families. Of course, it's not homework in the traditional sense of the word. With the overwhelming research on the importance of reading to children and the research supporting the need for parent involvement in the child's education, these packs are simple yet effective tools. Each "pack" contains a storybook for the family to keep and a page of activity ideas for the families to complete together at home. Sometimes there might be an activity that the families are asked to bring back to school, with no particular deadline given, but mostly there is no need for families to prove that they've completed the activities.

Parent-only Activities

Some nature-based preschools have had great success with parent-only social activities. These give the parents an opportunity to build their support network in the community. A nice sit-down dinner, wine tasting, or dessert night are popular activities. These evenings can also be combined with an auction (live and/or silent) and function as a fundraiser. I've seen a school fundraiser where dinner is a little fancier with a donation level cost per plate, a live auction, and then silent auction baskets created by each classroom. Most parents are happy to donate funds to your program, and even happier if they get to have a little fun as well. Of course, be sure to keep your families in mind. If a fundraiser would be financially stressful for your families, focus on the fun, social events that don't have a cost. Any activity you do as a preschool should support your program, which means focusing on the kids and their families needs first.

Communication with Parents

Another way parents can be involved is to be aware of what's happening in the child's school day. If a parent knows that the child went in search of insects today, they can have a more meaningful and engaging conversation with that child about his/her day.

A weekly or monthly schedule of activities is a must for any preschool. At CNC we do a weekly schedule, which allows us to include a little more detail and we're not committed to an activity three weeks from now. This allows for more real-world happenings to be incorporated. Whatever the length of time covered, share what hikes the class will be going on, the books you plan to read in the class, the songs they'll be singing, and so forth. If you have room it's nice to include the lyrics to songs. After all, we've all experienced a "What are you saying?" or "Where did you learn that?" moment with children.

It's also good to have a monthly newsletter to share information relevant to all of the classes. The newsletter should include logistical information like upcoming days off school, reminders about bringing in extra clothes, checking the lost and found, etc. Photos of the preschoolers are a huge hit anywhere they appear, but particularly in the newsletter. Include as many as you possibly can! The newsletter is also a place for parent education. Provide an article or two each month on your teaching philosophy or things parents can do at home. At CNC some of the articles we've included have been on why nature-based education is beneficial, process versus project art, maple syrup recipes for parents to try with their kids, how to engage your kids at the dinner table to share about their day, and more.

These written materials can be emailed home to families or placed in a classroom mailbox for them to pick up each day of preschool. You have to do what is best for your families. That may mean doing a combination of email and hard copies. Whatever the method, be sure your parents have access to these resources. This includes posting the lesson plans and newsletter in the preschool building. There's no guarantee parents will read the materials, but you have to make it as available to them as possible. Many programs have a password-protected website where families can go for information. Be careful with social networking sites, as they can make it difficult to maintain privacy for the children and families.

Nature Center Membership—Maintaining the Connection

Any nature center with a nature-based preschool will tell you that it's vital to make families feel part of the greater nature center family and to maintain that connection after the children have moved on to kindergarten. This connection is built in many ways, such as the preschool building itself being in close proximity to the visitor center. Another significant way is nature center membership—to ensure that families continue receiving communication and discounts to programming. Most nature-based preschools make sure preschool families are members of the nature center while they're in school. Some require membership in order to register for the program, and others include membership as part of the tuition. While there's a procedural difference both methods are ensuring that families are members while enrolled.

The trick, of course, is maintaining membership after families have left. Hopefully you've created a positive enough experience through preschool and their participation in your other programs throughout the year that they'll choose to remain members. Just in case, however, some nature centers give families a complimentary six-month membership on the last day of the child's preschool experience.

Alumni events are another way to help keep families involved. There's no surefire way to keep families engaged in the nature center over time, but it's vital that you do everything you can. After all, these are families who have had a significant life-changing experience at your center. If you've done any friend- or fundraising you know that means they're prime candidates to be significant supporters in the long run.

6

Perfecting the Program

Congratulations! Your program is up and running and things are starting to operate like a well-oiled machine. Unfortunately, your work isn't done. In fact, it's never really done. This is the time to focus on perfecting the details of your program, and take it from a good program to an outstanding one. This generally means looking for support and information from outside your organization.

Professional Development for Teachers

Speaking of investing in the long-term success of your program, I encourage you to invest as much as possible in the professional development of your program staff. There will be licensing requirements for professional development that you will have to meet. However, that's the minimum you should be providing for your teachers. We all know that in order to grow and challenge the status quo, we need to be exposed to new ideas, the latest research, and other people doing the same kind of work we're doing.

Finding the perfect professional development opportunities for nature-based preschool teachers can be a challenge. After all, nature-based preschools activities are very different from traditional preschools activities that are typically being shared at early childhood conferences. A preschool of this kind is also different from the work most environmental educators are doing. In fact, the needs of nature-based preschool teachers are unique enough that there are plans in the works, as of this printing, to have a conference specifically for nature-based preschool teachers. In the meantime, there are benefits in learning in both realms of education. There are great resources and teachers out there—it's just a matter of finding them. In other words, don't give up on providing professional development for your teachers because there isn't one perfect conference to attend each year. You may find that your staff has different needs and should attend different conferences. For example, a teacher with an early childhood background might benefit most from an environmental education training, whereas someone with environmental education background might benefit most from an early childhood conference.

Early Childhood Specialist

An early childhood specialist is a consultant that has more training and/or experience than your staff. Generally this should be someone with a master's degree and several years teaching experience. Some communities have a person like this on staff in the local school district. If you don't have that in your community, you may need to turn to someone at the university level.

Essentially, you're looking for someone with a strong background in early childhood education who can objectively critique your program to help you move forward. The specialist will observe a program or two in action and provide feedback on the teacher and child interactions, flow of the daily schedule, materials in the classroom, and more. The person is looking to see that you're implementing early childhood best practices in every way possible. Think of this person as a coach or mentor.

As I mentioned, this person is a consultant. In other words, you'll have to allocate money in your budget to have this person visit your site and then provide both verbal and written feedback. I recommend that you have this person visit your site three times in a year. At minimum, they should visit twice per year to allow you to improve on suggestions made at the first visit and provide feedback on those improvements after the second visit. I realize this poses a financial burden, but this is an investment in the long-term quality of your program, and will pay dividends over time. If you are receiving funding from an outside source, they may actually require you to have this independent program review and assessment process in place. In Michigan, for example, the state funded Great Start Readiness Programs are required to have an early childhood specialist assigned to their program.

Program Assessment

We'd all love to say, "Our program is great," but how do we know that's true? Well, this is where overall program assessment is useful. Program assessment looks at the overall package that is your preschool—teachers, facilities, daily schedule, parent involvement, etc. One widely used program assessment is the High Scope Foundation's Preschool Program Quality Assessment, commonly called the "PQA." Another tool that more and more states are using is the Quality Improvement Rating System (QRIS). This tool rates a program's performance and outlines a plan for improvement to move to the next rating level. Most likely, your community and state have a tool that is preferred. It doesn't matter which tool you're using, but just that you're using one.

You'll want to complete the assessment as a self-evaluation, but it's also important to have an outside person complete the assessment as well. If you seek out an early childhood specialist, this is the ideal person to complete the assessment. It will also allow you to see how you compare to other programs in your community. It's easy to get caught up in the hustle and bustle of day-to-day tasks and forget to look at the big picture. It's vital to improvement and progress that, at least annually, you stop and evaluate your overall program.

Accreditation

The National Association for the Education of Young Children (NAEYC) is a national organization that sets standards for quality programming for birth through eight years of age. NAEYC coordinates an accreditation program as a way for a preschool to show parents, community members, and other professionals that the program meets quality standards.

Currently there are four primary steps to accreditation: 1) enrollment and self-study; 2) application/self-assessment; 3) candidacy; and 4) site visit. Accreditation is an involved and time-consuming process that many programs choose not to pursue. However, it is essential for raising the quality of early childhood education in our individual communities and across the country. New Canaan Nature Center Preschool and Dodge Nature Preschool are accredited nature-based preschools. Schlitz Nature Preschool is currently in the process and expects to be accredited in 2012. Chippewa Nature Center expects to begin the process in another year or two.

For more information on NAEYC accreditation visit www.naeyc.org/accreditation.

7

The Next Step—Moving Nature-Based Preschools Forward on a Larger Scale

There are more than twenty nature-based preschools currently operating in the United States. Those numbers have been steadily growing over the last few years, and hopefully will continue to grow. However, to be truly successful as a concept and program model there are a few things we need to do. When I say "we" I mean those of us operating or working for a nature-based preschool, and those who support these programs.

To be successful on a grand scale, I believe we need to: 1) share our program model with traditional preschools; 2) be advocates for nature-based play in all aspects of our communities, states, and country; 3) establish and maintain best practices for nature-based preschools; and 4) conduct research on the outcomes of nature-based preschools.

Share the Wealth

Nature-based preschools are unique, powerful, and effective models of education. However, as I mentioned in Chapter 2, there is no reason these programs have to occur only at nature centers. Any preschool in the country, even in an urban area, can implement the principles of nature-based preschools. Those of us in the choir, so to speak, now have the job of sharing the wealth with other preschools in our communities and states.

Some of this sharing of knowledge and ideas has already begun. At CNC we've started a summer "Nature Preschool Institute" where teachers attend a four-day workshop to learn about the program. Included in this workshop are three half-days of observing the program in action with kids and teachers in a regular school day session. Dodge Nature Preschool in Minnesota offers a learning conference, which is a one-day experience for preschool teachers to learn about the Dodge program and local natural history. They've also written an activity book, *Four Seasons at a Nature-Based Preschool*, which provides seasonal activity ideas. Schlitz Nature Preschool has created brain development cards, *Naturally Developing Young Brains*, which include a nature-based activity on one side of the card with a fact on the other side explaining the developmental value of that activity. Schlitz Nature Preschool will also be offering a "Nature Preschool Study Tour" for teachers beginning in the fall of 2011. They're also in the process of writing a nature-based curriculum. These are all great examples of sharing the wealth. We need even more.

Nature-based preschools shouldn't be rare gems scattered about the country—they should be everywhere. The philosophy behind a nature-based preschool such as daily outdoor experiences, awareness of seasonal changes, and developing a sense of place should be in every preschool across the country—whether or not they call themselves nature-based. For example, wouldn't it be great if every preschool in your community was taking children outside every day no matter how rainy or cold it might be? For that to become a reality we have to give preschool teachers the tools for success. Those tools range across a wide spectrum—from research supporting the developmental value to teaching the teachers themselves how to dress for the weather.

To see this vision become reality will take regular interactions with your fellow preschool professionals. Conversations will lead to trainings, which will lead to site visits to help a preschool revise its play area. Offer to give presentations at conferences. Suggest a natural history training as a professional development opportunity in your community. Write articles for early childhood professional newsletters, magazines, blogs, etc. Do whatever makes sense for your community to engage as many professionals as possible in play-based, outdoor-based, early childhood education. We want to protect the planet by building outdoor connections, and while doing so, we'll be saving childhood for our children.

Be an Advocate

This is really an extension of sharing the wealth. By being an advocate we're moving the nature-based philosophy outside the world of preschools. This means communicating the program value to community members, business leaders, and political leaders. This needs to happen at the local, state, and national level. It also means talking about our program models in their philosophical form so elements can be applied to education beyond early childhood.

Why is this necessary? Well, one of the big reasons is funding. We all know that financial support is critical to any program's success. Individual donors, corporate donors, and lawmakers can all have influence over your financial success. Another big reason relates to policy. Lawmakers and educational leaders have great impact on the daily operations of a preschool program—think of how many times I mentioned licensing in this book. If policy makers understand the educational value of a pile of logs in a play area they don't seem nearly as "dangerous." These factors come together when a private foundation offers grants for playground improvements and someone requests money to naturalize their playground. If the funders don't see the value in a natural play area, and see them as hazards rather than assets, that grant is sure to be denied. However, if they're educated on the value and benefits, the funder will be more likely to support the efforts.

Essentially by being advocates we're shifting the cultural thinking to include regular outdoor play at all levels of education—a core value of all nature-based preschool programs.

Establish Best Practices

At the core of any profession is a set of standards, minimum expectations—or in other words, best practices. While there are best practices in place for early childhood education and standards for environmental education at the early childhood level, there aren't standards for nature-based preschools.

Should a program be called nature-based just because it's located in the woods? No, that alone is not enough. Does time outside on the plastic climbing structure count as a meaningful outdoor experience? Not by my definition. The point is there are a range of programs in operation. If we are going to be taken seriously as we share the wealth and advocate we need to have a list of professional standards that we adhere to which we adhere.

Patti Bailie, director of the Schlitz Nature Preschool in Milwaukee, has done extensive research as part of her doctoral dissertation on the existing nature-based preschools. She has visited many schools and interviewed the directors at those sites. Patti has also been one of the foremost leaders in the nature-based preschool movement for more than a decade. This is my public appeal for her to compile her research and experience, or at least to jump start the discussion on establishing best practices for nature-based preschools. However, the burden of establishing best practices isn't Patti's to carry. If we are to call ourselves professionals we should all be asking ourselves what it is that makes a quality nature-based preschool. How are we different from traditional preschools? What makes us uniquely us? What should be minimum standards for nature-based preschool operations? How do we measure success? In other words, if we're striving for excellence, what does excellence look like in practice? The only way we can achieve excellence is to continually ask these questions.

Support Research

The last, but by no means least, thing we need to be concerned about is research. Longitudinal studies would be ideal. We need scientific research, quantitative and qualitative, on the outcomes of nature-based preschools.

There is extensive research on the value of preschool—from immediate outcomes to long-term benefits of investing in early childhood education. There is also more and more research emerging on the positive effects of outdoor time on children. However, we haven't done research on nature-based preschools specifically. How do children compare to their counterparts at a traditional preschool? There is lots of anecdotal evidence, but when it comes down to it—anecdotes won't pay the bills.

The possibilities for research are numerous. What are the effects of daily outdoor experiences on a preschooler? Do these experiences have an impact on the various developmental domains (physical, cognitive, social-emotional)? What role does the play area have in developing these domains? What is the "ideal" natural play area for preschoolers? There are people doing research, and I applaud these folks. Robin Moore of North Carolina State University, for example, has done extensive studies on play areas. Frances Kuo and her team at the University of Illinois have been studying the role of nature in children's lives for years. Ruth Wilson, professor emeritus at Bowling Green State University, focused much of her research on early childhood environmental education. However, I think Moore, Kuo, and Wilson would all agree that there is a need for even more research.

If we're going to have a serious and solid position in the early childhood profession we need concrete evidence that nature-based preschools impact child learning outcomes. There is more and more pressure to make every moment impactful in the education world. If we are to expect early childhood educators to adopt the nature-based approach, we have to have evidence that it's as or more effective than the currently accepted best practices. The research to date could lead one to assume that nature-based preschools have a significant positive effect on young children, but it's time for us to be able to say that with scientific certainty.

A

Appendix: Resources for Research Related to Nature-Based Preschools

Early Childhood Data

Child Trends DataBank. www.childtrendsdatabank.org
KIDS COUNT Census Data. www.kidscount.org/census
National Association of Child Care Resource & Referral Agencies (NACCRRA). www.naccrra.org/randd
National Center for Education Statistics. nces.ed.gov
National Institute for Early Education Research. www.nierr.org

Benefits of Nature Play

Children & Nature Network. www.childrenandnature.org/research.
This site has many fantastic resources on research related to children and nature. In September 2009 Children & Nature Network published Research and Studies: Volume Four, *which is the updated version in a series of annotated bibliographies on research related to children's time in nature—a highly recommended report!*

Recommended Reading

Brett, A. & Moore, R. 1993. *The Complete Playground Book.* New York: Syracuse University Press.

Gil, E. 1991. *The Healing Power of Play.* New York: Guilford Press.

Louv, R. 2005. *Last Child in the Woods: Saving Our Children from Nature-Deficit Disorder.* Chapel Hill, NC: Algonquin Press.

Louv, R. 2011. *The Nature Principle.* Chapel Hill, NC: Algonquin Press.

Moore, R. & Wong, H. 1997. *Natural Learning: The Life History of an Environmental Schoolyard.* Berkeley, CA: MIG Communications.

Moore, R. Goltsman, S & Iacofano, D. (Eds., second edition). 1992. *The Play For All Guidelines: Planning, Design, and Management of Outdoor Play Settings For All Children.* Berkeley, CA: MIG Communications.

Myers, G. 1998. *Children and Animals: Social Development and our Connections to Other Species.* Boulder, CO: Westview Press.

Nicholson, S. 1971. The Theory of Loose Parts. *Landscape Architecture,* 62(1), 30-34.

Rivkin, R. 1995. *The Great Outdoors: Restoring Children's Right to Play Outdoors.* Washington, D.C.: NAEYC.

United Nations 1989. *The Convention on the Rights of the Child.* New York: UNICEF.

Westland, C. & Knight, J. 1982. *Playing, Living, Learning: A Worldwide Perspective on Children's Opportunities to Play.* State College, PA: Venture Publishing.

Wilson, R. 2008. *Nature and Young Children: Encouraging Creative Play and Learning in Natural Environments.* New York: Routledge.

B

Appendix: Programming Resources

It would be impossible to list every possible resource related to nature-based preschools, early childhood education, and environmental education. However, below are a few of the "must-visit" websites related to nature-based preschools.

Nature-Based Preschools

Chippewa Nature Center's Nature Preschool, Midland, MI. chippewanaturecenter.org/naturepreschool.htm

Dodge Nature Preschool, West St. Paul, MN. dodgenaturecenter.org/Preschool

Kalamazoo Nature Center's Nature's Way Preschool, Kalamazoo, MI. naturecenter.org/Preschool.aspx

New Canaan Nature Center Preschool, New Canaan, CT. www.newcanaannature.org

Schlitz Audubon Nature Preschool, Milwaukee, WI. www.sanc.org/natpre.htm

Curricula & Assessment

Creative Curriculum.® www.teachingstrategies.com

Reggio-Emilia. www.reggioalliance.org (in the U.S.)

High Scope Foundation. www.highscope.org

Furniture

Community Playthings. www.communityplaythings.com

Environments. www.eichild.com

General Supplies

Discount School Supply. www.discountschoolsupply.com
Lakeshore. www.lakeshorelearning.com

Nature-specific Supplies

Acorn Naturalists. www.acornnaturalists.com
Carolina Biological. www.carolina.com
Crazy Crow Trading Post. www.crazycrow.com (a great source for animal furs)
BioQuip. www.bioquip.com (a great source for pond dippers)
Forestry Suppliers. www.forestry-suppliers.com
Skulls Unlimited. www.skullsunlimited.com
Nature Watch. nature-watch.com
Outdoor Adventure Kid Company. www.oakiwear.com (a fantastic source for child-size rain suits)

Play Area Development

North Carolina State University's Natural Learning Institute. www.naturalearning.org (design ideas, research, and resources)
Earthplay. www.planetearthplayscapes.com (design and supplies)
Nature Explore www.arborday.org/explore (design and supplies)
Green Hearts, Inc. www.greenheartsinc.org (design suggestions)

Nature-based Early Childhood Activities

Cornell, J. 1979. *Sharing Nature with Children*. Nevada City, CA: Dawn Publications.

Danks, F. & Scofield, J. 2007. *Nature's Playground: Activities, Crafts, and Games to Encourage Children to Get Outdoors*. Chicago: Chicago Review Press.

Dodge Nature Preschool. [Year]. *Four Seasons at a Nature Based Preschool*. West Saint Paul, MN: Dodge Nature Center. Available for purchase at www.dodgenaturecenter.org/Preschool.

Drake, J. 2001. *The Kids Winter Handbook*. Tonawanda, New York: Kids Can Press.

Lingelbach, J. & Purcell, L. Eds. 2000. *Hands-On Nature: Information and Activities for Exploring the Environment with Children*. Woodstock, VT: Vermont Institute of Natural Science.

Schlitz Audubon Nature Preschool's activity cards. *Naturally Developing Young Brains.* Available for purchase at www.braininsightsonline.com.

Schiller, P. 2006. *Bountiful Earth: 25 Songs and Over 300 Activities for Young Children.* Silver Spring, MD: Gryphon House.

Professional Associations

National Association for the Education of Young Children. www.naeyc.org
North American Association for Environmental Education. www.naaee.org
National Association for Interpretation. www.interpnet.com

C

Appendix: Recommended Children's Books

There are many, many great children's books out there. When you're starting a nature-based preschool library the choices can be overwhelming. To help simplify the process a bit the teachers at Chippewa Nature Center's Nature Preschool have selected a few of their favorites. Here is their list:

Birds

Aston, D. 2006. *An Egg is Quiet.* San Francisco, CA: Chronicle Books.

Gallo, F. & Lohstoeter, L. 2001. *Bird Calls* (Hear and There Books). Norwalk, CT: Innovative Kids.

Wood, A. 1997. *Bird Songs.* Boston: Harcourt Children's Books.

Winer, Y. 2002. *Birds Build Nests.* Watertown, MA: Charlesbridge.

Ehlert, L. 1996. *Feathers for Lunch.* Riverside, UT: Sandpiper.

Body Awareness

Baptiste, B. 2004. *My Daddy is a Pretzel: Yoga for Parents and Kids.* Cambridge, MA: Barefoot Books.

Diversity

Lionni , L. 2006. *A Color of His Own.* New York: Knopf Books for Young Readers.

LaVigna Coyle, C. 2003. *Do Princesses Wear Hiking Boots?* Lanham, MD: Cooper Square.

Howe, J. 1994. *I Wish I Were a Butterfly.* Riverside, UT: Sandpiper.

Fact Books

Various books by Llewellyn, C.: *Starting Life Butterfly; Starting Life Duck; Starting Life Frog; Starting Life Ladybug.*

Family

Penn, A. 2006. *Kissing Hand.* Terre Haute, IN: Tanglewood Press.*

Field Guides

Stokes, D. 1996. *Stokes Beginner's Guide to Birds: Eastern Region.* New York: Little, Brown and Company.

Various books by Burnie, D.: Smithsonian. *Bird Watcher* and *Smithsonian Bug Hunter.*

In addition, look for field guides specific to your region.

Fields

Fleming, D. 1995. *In The Tall Tall Grass.* New York: Henry Holt and Co.

Keats, E.J. 1999. *Over in the Meadow.* London: Puffin.

Forest

Pfeffer, W. 2007. *A Log's Life.* New York: Aladdin.

Friendship

Schubert, I. & Schubert, D. 2001. *Beaver's Lodge.* Smyrna, TN: Lemniscaat USA.

Various books by Lionni, L.: *Fish is Fish* and *It's Mine!*

Pinkney, J. 2009. *The Lion and the Mouse.* New York: Little, Brown Books for Young Readers

Herps

Kalan, R. 2004. *Jump, Frog, Jump.* Pine Plains, NY: Live Oak Media.

Invertebrates

Various books by Allen, J.: *Are you an Ant?; Are you a Bee?; Are you a Butterfly?*

Various books by Rockwell, A.: *Becoming Butterflies* and *Bugs are Insects.*

Shields, C. 2002. *The Bugliest Bug.* Somerville, MA: Candlewick Press.

Ryder, J. 1988. *The Snail's Spell.* London: Puffin.

Frederick, A.D. 2001. *Under One Rock: Bugs, Slugs, and other Ughs.* Nevada City, CA: Dawn Publications.

Various books by Carle, E.: *Very Clumsy Click Beetle* and *The Very Quiet Cricket.*

Mammals

McLoskey, R. 1976. *Blueberries For Sal.* New York: Viking Press.

Rosen, M. 2009. *We're Going on a Bear Hunt.* New York: Margaret K. McElderry Books.

Miscellaneous

McCarthy, M. 2007. *A Closer Look.* New York: Greenwillow Books.

Christian, P. 2008. *If You Find a Rock.* Riverside, UT: Sandpiper.

Portis, A. 2006. *Not a Box.* New York: Harper Collins.

Portis, A. 2007. *Not a Stick.* New York: Harper Collins.

Night

Frank Gallo, F. 2001. *Night Sounds* (Play the Sounds, Pull the Tabs). South Norwalk, CT: Innovative Kids.

Pond

George, L. 1996. *Around the Pond: Who's Been Here.* New York: Greenwillow Books.

Fleming, D. 2007. *In The Small Small Pond.* New York: Henry Holt and Co.

Seasons

Bear Snores On (and other books) by Karma Wilson

By Julia Rawlinson: *Fletcher and the Falling Leaves* and *Fletcher and the Springtime Blossoms.*

George, L. 1999. *In the Snow: Who's Been Here*. New York: Greenwillow Books.

Ray, M. L. 2001. *Mud*. Riverside, UT: Sandpiper.

Hunter, A. 1998. *Possum's Harvest Moon*. Riverside, UT: Sandpiper.

Ehlert, L. 1999. *Snowballs*. Riverside, UT: Sandpiper.

Haas, J. 1996. *Sugaring*. New York: Greenwillow Books.

Chall, M. 2000. *Sugarbush Spring*. New York: Harper Collins.

Stewart, M. 2009. *Under the Snow*. Atlanta, GA: Peachtree Publishers.

Laan, N. 2000. *When Winter Comes*. New York: Atheneum/Anne Schwartz Books.

Stewardship

Mazer, A. 1994. *The Salamander Room*. Decorah, IA: Dragonfly Books.*

McGinty, A. 2007. *Thank You World*. New York: Dial.

Trees and Leaves

Gerber, C. 2006. *Leaf Jumpers*. Watertown, MA: Charlesbridge Publishing.

Zweibel, A. 2007. *Our Tree Named Steve*. London: Puffin.

*These books are given to students upon enrollment in CNC's Nature Preschool.

D

Appendix: Lead Teacher Job Description

In 2007 Chippewa Nature Center hired its first lead teacher for Nature Preschool. Below are the duties, responsibilities, and qualifications that were listed in the original job posting.

Objective: To maintain a developmentally appropriate classroom within the philosophical guidelines of the Nature Preschool and the Creative Curriculum® model, in order to develop students' relationship with the natural world.

Duties and Responsibilities

1. Teach and develop curriculum of Nature Preschool in conjunction with other members of the teaching team.
2. Assure that classroom operates within the guidelines and standards of the National Academy of Early Childhood Programs; the Michigan Department of Human Services, Office of Children and Adult Licensing; and the Michigan Department of Education's School Readiness Program.
3. Responsible for the health, safety, and welfare of all children in the group.
4. Conduct regular assessment of children and the overall program.
5. Conduct home visits and parent teacher conferences.

6. Train and supervise all paraprofessional support staff for his/her classroom in conjunction with the director of education.
7. Overall planning for equipment and supply needs in conjunction with assistant teacher.
8. Work with parents both formally and informally, individually and in groups.
9. Involvement in development, implementation, and review of Nature Preschool policies, procedures, and activities in conjunction with the CNC director of education and the WMFC director of programs.
10. Assist with the development and implementation of early childhood Nature Day Camp programs in the summer.
11. Other duties as assigned.

Qualifications:

1. Valid Michigan teaching certificate with a ZA endorsement or CDA; or bachelor's degree in child development with a focus on preschool.
2. One to five years teaching experience preferred.
3. Must have the knowledge of principles and techniques of early childhood education and developmentally appropriate practice and the ability to implement that knowledge.
4. Knowledge of and experience with environmental education and related curricula (i.e., Project WILD)
5. Experience with Creative Curriculum® preferred.
6. Experience with child and program assessment.
7. Must have the creativity, flexibility, and understanding necessary for working with children, parents, and coworkers.
8. Effective verbal and written communication skills.
9. Ability to solve practical problems.
10. Computer literacy including working knowledge of Windows platform and Microsoft Office software package.
11. Certification in child and adult CPR and basic first aid.

About the Author

Rachel Larimore is the director of education at the Chippewa Nature Center (CNC). She has been with CNC since 2001, and her duties include coordinating all youth programs (school programs, nature day camp, scouts, nature preschool, etc). She implemented all of the on-the-ground work to take the Nature Preschool from a vision to a reality in 2007—a program that now serves more than eighty three- and four-year-old children. She also co-chaired the nature center's $6 million expansion project, which was completed in 2010. In addition to renovations to the visitor center, the expansion included an approximately 5,000-square-foot preschool building. Rachel received a M.A. in park and recreation administration from Central Michigan University and B.S. in natural resource recreation and tourism, with an emphasis in interpretation, from Colorado State University. Raised on a vegetable farm in central Illinois, Rachel knows first hand the positive impact that nature plays in a child's development.